MEDAL OF HONOR
ALLIED ASSAULT
SPEARHEAD
EXPANSION PACK

PRIMA'S OFFICIAL STRATEGY GUIDE

DAVID KNIGHT

Prima Games
A Division of Random House, Inc.
3000 Lava Ridge Court
Roseville, CA 95661
1-800-733-3000
www.primagames.com

PRIMA'S OFFICIAL STRATEGY GUIDE

Associate Product Manager: Christy L. Curtis
Project Editor: Teli Hernandez

All products and characters mentioned in this book are trademarks of their respective companies.

Important:
Prima Games has made every effort to determine that the information contained in this book is accurate. However, the publisher makes no warranty, either expressed or implied, as to the accuracy, effectiveness, or completeness of the material in this book; nor does the publisher assume liability for damages, either incidental or consequential, that may result from using the information in this book. The publisher cannot provide information regarding game play, hints and strategies, or problems with hardware or software. Questions should be directed to the support numbers provided by the game and device manufacturers in their documentation. Some game tricks require precise timing and may require repeated attempts before the desired result is achieved.

ISBN: 0-7615-4004-0
Library of Congress Catalog Card Number: 2002114015

Printed in the United States of America
02 03 04 05 BB 10 9 8 7 6 5 4 3 2 1

Acknowledgements

There are a number of people I'd like to recognize for making this project a reality. First, I'd like to thank Christy Curtis and Teli Hernandez at Prima Games for their assistance, patience, and diligent work. I'd also like to thank Lincoln Herschberger, Brady Bell, Jon Galvan, and Dave Nash at Electronic Arts for their valuable input and cooperation. Finally, I'd like to thank my brother Michael whose advice and encouragement kept me focused and optimistic.

Contents

Congratulations on your purchase of *Medal of Honor Allied Assault Spearhead: Prima's Official Strategy Guide*. You are now equipped take on the worst that the enemy can throw at you.

Spearhead is our next chapter in the Medal of Honor Allied Assault universe. As Sergeant Jack Barnes of the 501st Parachute Infantry Regiment, you are called upon to lead, survive, sacrifice, and ultimately, trail-blaze a path to a total Allied victory. You will be among the first to set foot on enemy soil and among the few to witness the final death throws of the Third Reich. Fighting alongside British and Soviet troops, you will learn how to master a new arsenal of weapons in your penultimate fight against Axis tyranny. Your journey will take you from the skies over occupied France to the center of war-torn Berlin: the heart and soul of the evil German war machine. It's up to you to determine the outcome.

In multiplayer, *Spearhead* introduces our new Tug of War mode (TOW). Here, individual achievement is left behind and only those players who work with their teammates will succeed. Learn the strengths of your squad, balance your weapons, and you'll crush your enemies.

In the following pages you will gain vital knowledge that will assist in your campaign. Remember what you learn, and you will have the advantage over your opponent.

On behalf of the development team, thank you for your patronage and support of Medal of Honor.

Brady Bell
Producer
Electronic Arts Los Angeles

1
BASIC TRAINING

Listen up, soldier! As a veteran of the *Allied Assault* campaigns, you probably feel you don't need a refresher course in combat basics. But the enemies waiting in the campaigns ahead aren't rusty like you. As the war draws to a foreseeable end, the German forces have their backs against the wall, prompting them to lash out with every nasty surprise they can muster. If you thought the enemy was fierce before, you haven't seen anything yet. Remember, you're invading their home turf and they have nothing to lose. They'll exploit every opportunity to gun you down like the maggot you are! So wipe that know-it-all grin off your face and fall in…it's time for basic training!

Movement

Your survival and success as an infantry soldier depend on your ability to maneuver. That may sound like a no-brainer, but knowing how and where to move means the difference between evading enemy fire and catching a mouthful of lead from a concealed machine gun nest. Furthermore, studying the basics of movement proves useful on the battle field, yielding a variety of tactical opportunities.

Running and Walking

The default method of moving is running. Run by pressing the forward movement key (default W).

The fast pace of the game requires more running than walking.

2

Use the mouse to control direction and pitch. Although this is the fastest way to move across terrain, it's also the loudest. Your enemies are eerily perceptive and hear your boots striking the ground long before you come into sight. The game is hard enough without announcing your presence to every nearby enemy.

TIP

Firing weapons while moving decreases your accuracy. Instead, fire from a stationary position, preferably from behind cover.

For a stealthier approach, walk. Obviously, this is slower than running, but it also produces less sound, allowing you to sneak around. For example, by walking you can sometimes sneak into rooms without being detected. This gives you a significant advantage over busting into a room with guns blazing. To walk, press left (Shift) when moving. Walking is quieter than running, but it doesn't make you invisible. Don't expect to go undetected by walking—you'll need to use cover, too.

Strafing

Strafing (or side stepping) is the single most important method of movement you need to master as a front line soldier. Strafing allows you to move laterally without changing your facing direction. You can strafe left by pressing (A) and right with (D). Strafe left and right while using the mouse to stay focused on one point. There are

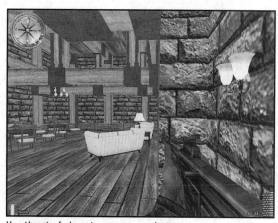

Use the strafe keys to move around corners.

numerous applications for this maneuver. Here's a list of ways to use strafing to your advantage:

- Avoiding enemy fire
- Frustrating snipers with zigzagging movements
- Moving around corners
- Ducking in and out of cover

Circle-Strafing

Circle-strafing is a tactic that evolved from heated multiplayer sessions of early first-person shooters. It also has applications in single-player games—it drives the enemy AI mad! Use a strafe key to circle around a target while shooting. This makes you tougher to hit while exposing your target to continuous fire from multiple directions.

To practice circle-strafing, find a stationary object such as a table or chair. Use the mouse to position the object in the center of the screen. Now, press one of the strafe keys and move the mouse to compensate for your lateral movements to keep the object centered at all times. As long as you stay focused on the object, you'll travel in a full circle. Move in the other direction.

In the single-player campaigns, circle-strafing is a valuable tactic to use against stationary tanks. As their turrets rotate to track your movements, begin strafing around the tank. If you're close enough, you'll stay just ahead of the tank's main gun. But pay attention—if you circle too quickly the turret will change directions in an effort to outsmart you. So, always circle in the same direction as the turret's rotation and watch out for direction changes. This should buy you enough time to place an explosive charge and get away before it explodes.

Crouching

Crouch to crawl through small spaces and take cover from enemy fire. The crouch function works as a toggle between standing up and crouching. Press left Ctrl to initiate a crouched stance. You'll remain crouched until you press the same key again to stand up. Always be aware of which stance you're in. While crouched, you move slower

than when standing. If you
need to move quickly across
the enemy's field of fire, do it
while standing.

Crouching reduces your
profile, making you a smaller,
more compact target. This
is more effective if you
use proper cover for
concealment—the less
you expose to the enemy,
the smaller the target you
present. All sorts of objects
can be used for cover, the

Crouch behind rocks and trees for increased concealment.

most ideal being objects you can see over, allowing you to return
fire. Find solid objects such as rocks, stone walls, and mounds
of rubble.

Crouching behind cover is essential when using weapons with
scopes. While looking through a scope, you're vulnerable to attacks
from all directions because of the limited viewing arc. Even if you're
being sneaky, you may miss an unsuspecting target, causing him to
open fire in your direction. If this happens, you'll be happy you're
crouched behind something.

Jumping

With the exception of clearing
obstructing objects, jumping
serves no real tactical
function. Press (Spacebar) to
jump. The height you can
jump is limited. You can't leap
over tall walls or even low
fence lines—all that gear
you're carrying is heavy!
However, you can jump up
onto crates and other low
objects. Sometimes jumping
onto these objects offers

Jump on small objects like these crates to reach new areas.

access to an area you couldn't reach otherwise. But don't waste too much time exploring where you can and cannot jump. If jumping is required, it's clear.

Climbing

You'll need to climb and descend ladders to reach new areas. Like jumping, this is another intuitive method of movement that requires little tactical planning. Approach a ladder while pressing the move forward key ([W]) and use the mouse to look up. To descend a ladder, approach it and press the use key ([E]) to move onto it, then press the move forward key while looking down to descend.

Use caution when descending. If you don't press the use key to grab the ladder before moving down, you'll fall off, resulting in damage from the fall. Getting injured by falling off a ladder is embarrassing, so pay attention to what you're doing.

The Compass and Navigation

The compass helps guide you to your current objective.

To succeed in the missions, you need to go from one objective to the next expeditiously. If used properly, the compass will always keep you on track. Located in the top left corner of the screen, the compass provides the heading and approximate distance of your latest objective. The arrow on the outer rim indicates the heading of the objective. This arrow points to the top of the compass, you're now moving toward the objective. Distance to the objective is estimated by the two ball bearings on the outer rim, flanking each side of the heading arrow. As you get closer to the objective, the ball bearings will move closer together.

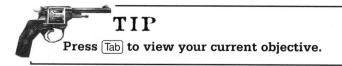

TIP

Press Tab to view your current objective.

Use the compass to provide a general direction to your next objective. However, pull your nose out of the compass and survey the battlefield before moving out. Your first priority is to secure safe passage, then concern yourself with navigation. The compass provides *as the crow flies* heading information, so you may need to actually move away from the compass heading to reach an objective. This is most common in urban settings where some paths or streets may be blocked by rubble or other obstacles. Finding another way around is pretty easy, but often involves engaging more enemies. So stay alert, soldier.

Weapons Training

For an infantry soldier, success on the battlefield means mastering a variety of weapons. We'll cover specific weapons in the next chapter. Before you get your hands on one, you'll need to learn how to use it.

Aiming

Aiming involves more than placing the crosshairs over an enemy and firing. You need to target specific areas of the enemy's body to take him down quickly. Doing so results in varying degrees of damage. For example, shooting at an enemy's arms and legs won't be lethal. It will take several hits in these areas before the enemy goes down. On the other hand, inflicting damage

Always aim for the torso. This guarantees a hit while inflicting serious damage on the target.

on the target's head or torso causes more damage and uses up less of your ammo in the process. Ideally, aim for the head every time. However, the head is a small target and it takes valuable time to line up properly in a heated firefight. Instead, aim for the torso, which offers the largest target area and is easy to see and hit at any range.

> ### TIP
> A single headshot usually takes down an enemy regardless of the weapon you're firing. But, on occasion, a bullet that strikes an enemy in the helmet may just knock it off his head. Follow through with more well-placed shots.

Things get more difficult when engaging moving targets. Don't aim where the enemy is, but where the enemy will be. This is called leading the target. By leading the target, you can place rounds in the path of their movement. If an enemy soldier moves from left to right, aim ahead of him to the right. With some practice (and a bit of luck), you'll successfully engage moving targets with relative ease.

> ### TIP
> Leading is most important when firing on fast-moving targets such as airplanes. From a fixed position on the ground, you won't be able to track an aircraft's movements across the sky fast enough to score direct hits. Instead, unleash a wall of lead directly in its flight path.

Firing

When dealing with semi-automatic or bolt-action rifles, firing is as easy as holding your aim and pulling the trigger (the left mouse button). The introduction of fully automatic weapons increases the learning curve substantially. Although these weapons can spit out a horrific amount of lead in a short time, their recoil sharply decreases your accuracy

Use short bursts when firing automatic weapons such as this tank-mounted machine gun.

the longer you hold down the trigger. Each time a single round is fired, the weapon jerks back, causing the muzzle to climb upward. By the time several rounds pass through the weapon, the aim will be far off the intended target. Furthermore, refocusing the weapon's aim becomes virtually impossible while it bucks out of control. To avoid this, fire automatic weapons with short, controlled bursts. This allows you to fire two or three rounds, adjust your aim, and fire again. You also expend less ammo and increase your accuracy.

Reloading

Have you ever entered a room full of enemies to discover that you only have two rounds left in your weapon? If you keep an eye on your ammo count and reload frequently, you won't have to worry about embarrassing situations like this.

Consider reloading your submachine guns after each engagement. Ammo for these weapons is relatively easy to find.

Most of the weapons in your arsenal hold eight to thirty rounds in a single magazine. Your ammo count is listed in the bottom right corner of the screen. Always inspect it before initiating any kind of attack. If your weapon is low on ammo, press R to reload. To be on the safe side, reload after any engagement, though this will also depend on the availability of ammo.

> ## TIP
> If you have to reload in a close combat situation, it's faster to change weapons instead. Either way, find cover or keep moving until you can open fire again.

9

Combat Tactics

During combat, tune out the surrounding chaos to focus on exploiting your enemy's weaknesses. Each combat situation is different, requiring quick analysis, improvisation, and action. However, with preparation you can rely on your training to take over when faced with particular challenges. Here are a few tactics to help overcome some of the more common obstacles facing you in the campaigns.

The Rifle Butt Strike

On rare occasions, you may run extremely low on ammo and need to take desperate measures. Fortunately, the rifle butt strike is an effective means of neutralizing enemies without expending ammo. However, you'll have to move into close combat range to perform this attack. Sneak up behind an enemy and strike him by pressing the secondary attack button (the right mouse button).

The rifle butt strike is an effective means of neutralizing the enemy during close combat.

If your enemy is already facing you, fire one or two rounds at his torso. This stuns him, giving you time to rush in and take him out. If he isn't stunned, he'll use this same tactic, too. Once an enemy is down, collect more ammo from him.

Popping Smoke

The addition of smoke grenades in the *Spearhead* expansion allows for creative and useful assault tactics. These grenades aren't used to choke up enemies, but rather to obscure their field of view. This makes them perfect to use against fixed enemy positions such as machine gun nests.

Unlike frag grenades, place the smoke somewhere between your position and the enemy's—don't throw it at the enemy. As the grenade bounces into place, it dispenses colored smoke. Wait until the smoke gets thick before using it for cover. Remember, smoke only makes it hard to see, it doesn't provide solid cover. Plan your movements and don't be too alarmed if you're hit by a lucky shot.

Placing smoke ahead of an advance helps hide your movements.

Smoke also can be used as a diversion. Because it's used to cover an advance, it draws the enemy's attention. Use this opportunity to approach from a different direction and catch the enemy by surprise. This tactic is just as useful in multiplayer games as it is in the single-player campaigns.

Shoot and Scoot

Shoot and scoot is a distraction tactic in which you use suppressing fire to advance on enemy positions. On missions where you're working with teammates (in single-player and multiplayer), move forward while your buddies open fire on the enemy. If they don't take out the enemy, at the very least they'll distract him while you move closer to engage.

The shoot and scoot tactic requires cooperation from your teammates.

This tactic relies on team coordination, but it's good to use when you're pinned down by enemy fire. To help cover your movements, throw a smoke grenade along your intended path.

Room Clearing

As you move into towns and cities, you'll have to root out enemy soldiers hiding in buildings. You'll move from room to room clearing each structure. This task is tedious and dangerous. To minimize the risks, never open doors and remain standing in the doorway—you'll make a nice juicy target.

Begin room entries with a quick grenade toss from the side of an open doorway.

Instead, open a door and immediately side step left or right. If there's no incoming fire or sounds from inside, side step in front of the doorway with an automatic weapon at the ready. Strafe until you gather as much information about the room as possible. Sweep each opposing corner without exposing yourself too much. By the time you finish sweeping the room, the only blind corners should be the ones on the other side of the adjacent wall. If you open a door and you hear sounds on the other side, toss in a grenade. Once it explodes, mow down any survivors with automatic fire. Depending on their proximity to the doorway, tossing a grenade into a room may draw enemies through the open door—be ready.

> ### TIP
> The shotgun is an excellent choice for room clearing. However, avoid using it in large rooms with multiple enemies. The pump-action delay between trigger pulls puts you at a tactical disadvantage.

12

Commendations

You're probably not in it for the glory, but it's still important to recognize individuals who rise above the call of duty. There are two types of medals awarded: Campaign Medals and Career Medals. Campaign Medals are awarded at the end of a successful campaign and can be seen in the bottom row of your medal case. Career Medals are awarded once all available campaigns are completed. These can be seen in the top row of the medal case. Below is a list of the medals awarded in the *Spearhead* expansion.

Campaign Medals

The France and Germany Star
Awarded by special circumstances from Great Britain for events surrounding June 6, 1944. This medal is awarded for successfully completing the Operation Overlord Campaign.

Belgian Croix De Guerre
Awarded by the Belgian nation in grateful recognition of service against an opposing armed force. This medal is awarded for successfully completing the Bastogne Campaign.

Medal for the Capture of Berlin
Awarded by the Soviet Red Army for extreme special circumstances. This medal is given for successfully completing the Berlin Campaign.

13

Career Medals

The Bronze Star

For meritorious achievement in service not involving aerial flight in operations against an opposing force. The Bronze Star is awarded for completing all the campaigns on Easy skill level.

The Silver Star

An award for gallantry in action against an opposing armed force. The Silver Star is awarded for completing all the campaigns on Medium skill level.

The Distinguished Service Cross

The second highest military award in the U.S. Armed Forces and given for extraordinary heroism in connection with military operations against an opposing force. The Distinguished Service Cross is awarded for completing all the campaigns on Hard skill level.

2
Weapons, Equipment, and Vehicles

soldier is only as good as his equipment, and the *Spearhead* expansion adds a number of new weapons and vehicles to an already impressive arsenal. This chapter looks at each weapon, providing historical information and tactical tips to make the most of each shot you take. We also cover the equipment needed to complete your varied mission objectives, plus tips for becoming familiar with the various vehicles you'll encounter on the battlefield. Some are friendly but most are gunning for you. Take some time to read up, soldier.

Pistols

Colt .45

Country of Origin: U.S.

Availability: Operation Overlord Campaign,
Assault in the Ardennes Campaign, Multiplayer

When the opposition gets close, grab your Colt .45. Reliable and accurate, the Colt .45 is the finest American military sidearm ever made. Each of the seven rounds in your clip can deliver lethal force against well-protected opposition. Just be careful, the kick is heavy.

Notes: For its small size, the Colt .45 packs a deadly punch. But like most pistols, it's only accurate at close range. Use it for close combat, but keep an eye on the ammo count—it can only hold seven rounds.

HISTORICAL NOTES: THE COLT .45

The Colt .45 was the sidearm of choice for the American military from 1911 until its retirement in 1984. Originally suspicious of its innovative auto loading mechanism, the American military asked its inventor, John M. Browning, to rework the mechanism before accepting the gun into service.

A subsequent version, the M1911A1, utilized recoil forces to push the slide back, eject the shell, cock the hammer, and reload the chamber within a fraction of a second. The finished version of this semiautomatic pistol packed more stopping power than its predecessor, the .38-cal M1900, and, with its improved autoloader, could fire at a more rapid rate. Although more than half of all enlisted men in World War I carried the Colt .45, regulations forbade infantrymen from using them in World War II. However, these regulations were rarely enforced, as many sought them as a weapon of last resort.

On VJ Day in 1945, the last order for Colt .45s was canceled by the U.S. military, and for the next 39 years all pistols in service were rehabilitated secondhands.

17

Walther P-38

Country of Origin: Germany

Availability: Multiplayer

The lean P-38 semiautomatic pistol is a weapon for the long hauls. Its reliable firing mechanism makes it a favorite among officers of the Wehrmacht.

Notes: This is a standard-issue sidearm usually found in the possession of German officers. Its eight-round capacity gives it a slight advantage over the other firearms in the pistol class.

Webley Revolver Mark IV

Country of Origin: U.K.

Availability: Operation Overlord Campaign, Multiplayer

Because of its considerable weight, the British Webley revolver Mark IV has very mild recoil. Despite the supposed limitations of revolver-class weapons with a break-open frame, the Webley is quite accurate and was produced out of a better quality steel than its predecessors.

Notes: This is the first revolver you'll come across and it's quite capable. Use it in small-scale firefights, or, if you're up for a challenge, use it to clear buildings.

7.62mm Model 1895 Nagant Revolver

Country of Origin: U.S.S.R.

Availability: The Fall of Berlin Campaign, Multiplayer

This is a unique Russian sidearm with a cylinder that rotates and is pushed forward so that the mouth of the cartridge actually enters the barrel. When the weapon is fired, the cartridge mouth expands and completely seals any gap for gasses to escape from the gun. A double-action configuration was given to all Soviet military personnel, who, in turn, found it a viable weapon to be fired out of the vision ports of their T34 tanks.

Notes: Although it's not the best weapon in your arsenal for city fighting, it can work in a pinch. If you plan on using it, make sure there's cover within reach. Like the Webley, and most other revolvers, you only have six shots, so make them count.

Rifles

M1 Garand

Country of Origin: U.S.

Availability: Operation Overlord Campaign, Assault in the Ardennes Campaign, Multiplayer

Popular for its caliber, muzzle velocity, and semiautomatic capabilities, the Garand has proven to be superior over earlier bolt-action rifles. However, its eight-round clip is impossible to reload when partially used; in the field, soldiers fire off all eight rounds before loading a fresh clip. When automatically emptying a spent clip, the M1 Garand emits a distinct "ping" sound.

Notes: Although it may not be as powerful as some of the rifles in its class, its semiautomatic function allows you to place several accurate shots in quick succession. By aiming at a target's torso, you can drop an enemy soldier with a couple of quick shots.

19

The M1 can't be reloaded during the middle of a clip—all eight rounds must be fired before the expended clip pops out, allowing you to load another. Despite this minor limitation, the M1 is still one of the best rifles available.

HISTORICAL NOTES: THE M1 GARAND

The U.S. Rifle, Caliber .30, M1 rifle, or Garand was the standard-issue rifle for American infantry. Named after its inventor, John C. Garand, it was the first semiautomatic rifle widely used in combat. Although it was adopted by the Army in 1936, the Garand was in short supply until 1943. By the end of the war, more than 4 million had been produced.

The Garand was easy to disassemble and clean, and its combination of caliber, muzzle velocity, and semiautomatic operation provided superior firepower over bolt-action rifles. Its only weakness was that partially fired clips were so difficult to reload, that GIs tended to simply fire off the remaining rounds before inserting a new clip.

Springfield '03 Sniper Rifle

Country of Origin: U.S.

Availability: Multiplayer

The internal magazine used in the Springfield 1903 sniper rifle is only five rounds, so snipers often use Colt .45s as sidearms in addition to carrying this weapon. Because the position of the scope significantly obstructs clip feed, rounds have to be inserted one at a time. This accurate weapon does expose you to return fire, so make your first shot count.

Notes: If this is your weapon of choice, only use it in situations where you're concealed and preferably far away from enemy forces. When moving from position to position, switch to your pistol, which offers better protection with its faster rate of fire.

Historical Notes: The Springfield '03 Sniper Rifle

Officially designated "U.S. Rifle, Caliber .30, Model of 1903," it was better known as the Springfield, the Springfield '03, or simply the '03. This bolt-action rifle was adopted by the U.S. Army in 1903 and remained the standard-issue rifle of America's armed forces until 1936.

In 1906, the .30-caliber cartridge was modified and designated the "M1906 Cartridge." It became widely known as the .30-06. This cartridge was the standard U.S. rifle and machine gun cartridge for the next 50 years.

In 1936, the Springfield '03 was replaced by the M1 Garand, but many Springfields saw service in World War II. In the Normandy Campaign, the Springfield was used primarily as a sniper weapon; the vast majority of infantrymen preferred semiautomatic and automatic weapons to the bolt-action rifle. Any advantage the Springfield may have had in accuracy was more than offset by the rate of fire the Garand, M1 Carbine, and Browning automatic rifle offered.

Mauser KAR98K

Country of Origin:
Germany

Availability: Assault in the
Ardennes Campaign, Multiplayer

This repeating rifle with a blunted nose is in the hands of all German soldiers for basic training. For many, it's their only weapon in combat and is useful in most situations.

Notes: Although it lacks the semiautomatic capability of its U.S. counterpart (the M1), this seemingly archaic bolt-action rifle is still a contender thanks to its incredible accuracy and range.

21

KAR98 Sniper Rifle

Country of Origin: Germany

Availability: Assault in
the Ardennes Campaign,
Multiplayer

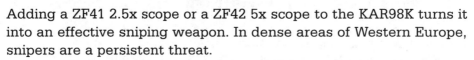

Adding a ZF41 2.5x scope or a ZF42 5x scope to the KAR98K turns it
into an effective sniping weapon. In dense areas of Western Europe,
snipers are a persistent threat.

Notes: This is the same rifle as the KAR98K, but with the addition of
a scope. The increased visibility offered by the scope allows skilled
snipers to utilize the full potential of the rifle's range and power.
This makes it the ideal weapon for defensive situations. Just make
sure you're well concealed.

Lee Enfield

Country of Origin:
U.K.

Availability: Operation Overlord
Campaign, Multiplayer

Having a long and distinguished evolution, the British Lee Enfield
rifle is a stalwart in the rifle class. The ten-round clip, bolt-action
rifle was an extremely accurate piece, without the harsh kickback of
equally high-velocity rifles.

Notes: After using the M1, switching to the Enfield may seem like a
step backward. In some respects, it is, but you'll begin to appreciate
the power and accuracy of this bolt-action rifle. Unlike
the M1, one shot from the Enfield is usually enough to take
down an enemy soldier. However, the long reloading
process can make you vulnerable to enemy fire.
Use the Enfield from covered
positions at long range.

Gewehr 43

Country of Origin: Germany

Availability: Assault in the Ardennes Campaign

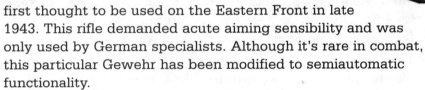

A logical evolution from the Gewehr 41, this telescopic rifle was first thought to be used on the Eastern Front in late 1943. This rifle demanded acute aiming sensibility and was only used by German specialists. Although it's rare in combat, this particular Gewehr has been modified to semiautomatic functionality.

Notes: The semiautomatic rate of fire coupled with the enhanced optics of a scope make this an awkward mix between a standard rifle and a sniper rifle. Still, you'll find this weapon useful for accurately taking out enemies from a distance. The disruptive recoil can make it hard to stay on target, but the more-than-adequate rate of fire makes up for this and any other shortcomings.

Mosin Nagant M1938 Carbine

Country of Origin: U.S.S.R.

Availability: The Fall of Berlin Campaign, Multiplayer

The Mosin Nagant was the first Russian rifle to incorporate the idea of a small-caliber, high-velocity magazine rifle.

Notes: Similar to the Lee Enfield and KAR98K, the Mosin Nagant is another high-powered, bolt-action rifle. Use this one at long range or whenever speedy reloading isn't an important factor. Only with the SVT 40 in your arsenal will the Nagant begin to feel obsolete.

23

SVT 40

Country of Origin:
U.S.S.R.

Availability: The Fall
of Berlin Campaign,
Multiplayer

The SVT 40 relied on gas operation with a locking
block cammed downward at the rear into a recess in the
receiver floor. It was characterized by the removal of the earlier
cleaning rod, with a more conventional position underneath the barrel.

Notes: This weapon is a bit like the Gewehr 43, sporting
semiautomatic fire and a scope. While moving through the rubble
filled streets of Berlin, you'll need to use this rifle to spot and
eliminate numerous enemy snipers. First, listen for enemy shots,
trying to determine their point of origin. Then look for muzzle
flashes. Once you have an idea where the sniper is, pull up the
scope to take him out. Never search for enemy snipers through the
scope view alone.

Submachine Guns

Thompson

Country of Origin: U.S.

Availability: Assault in
the Ardennes Campaign,
Multiplayer

Although many complain about the weight of the
Tommy Gun, it performs as designed: a rapid-firing,
sweep-and-clear weapon for close quarters. Its 30-round clip can
be emptied in less than three seconds.

Notes: Popularized by Prohibition-era gangsters in the U.S., the
Thompson's large caliber and automatic rate of fire also made it
a favorite of Allied soldiers. Compensate for the recoil by firing in
short, controlled bursts. Like most submachine guns, this one is
great for close combat tasks like clearing trenches.

HISTORICAL NOTES: THE THOMPSON SUBMACHINE GUN

John T. Thompson, who helped develop the Springfield '03 rifle and Colt .45 pistol, began work on a "trench broom" for close-quarters combat shortly after his retirement from the Army in 1918. He recognized that the .45-caliber slug of the M1911 pistol would be devastating when used in a fully automatic weapon. By the spring of 1920, Thompson's company (Auto-Ordnance) produced a prototype capable of firing 800 rounds per minute. Despite its excellent test performance, the Thompson was not adopted for use by either the U.S. Army or Marine Corps.

Still, Thompson contracted with Colt for the manufacture of 15,000 guns, designated "Thompson Submachine Gun, Model of 1921." The 15,000 guns manufactured by Colt lasted until the eve of World War II. In 1940, the U.S. Army ordered 20,000 Thompson submachine guns, and in 1941 the Army ordered an additional 319,000. One of the main assets of the Thompson submachine gun was reliability; it performed better than most submachine guns when exposed to dirt, mud, and rain. The complaints against the Thompson were its weight (over 10 pounds), its inaccuracy at ranges over 50 yards, and its lack of penetrating power (a common complaint with all World War II submachine guns).

MP-40

Country of Origin: Germany

Availability: Operation Overlord Campaign, Multiplayer

A simple technical innovation to the hammer eliminated the problems of the MP-38, and the MP-40 was born. Effective in close combat and clean in construction, the MP-40 is very cheap to make, as its parts are machine-stamped.

25

Notes: When no other submachine gun is available, the MP-40 can still deliver the automatic fire required by some combat situations. However, it isn't very accurate and lacks the stopping power offered by other weapons in this class. If multiple shots at close range fail to bring down an enemy, rush over and strike him with the weapon's butt while he's stunned. This should finish him off.

Sten Mark 2

Country of Origin: U.K.

Availability: Operation Overlord Campaign, Multiplayer

A lightweight and compact automatic weapon, the Sten Mark 2 was considered the workhorse of the British military, with more than two million produced in less than three years. It can hold as many as 32 rounds, but was generally loaded with 30 to avoid jamming and magazine spring complications.

Notes: For its simple and compact design, the Sten is a surprisingly effective weapon. The large spring inside absorbs most of the recoil, allowing you to stay on target through relatively long bursts of automatic fire. This makes it useful for engaging targets at both medium and close ranges.

PPSh41

Country of Origin: U.S.S.R.

Availability: The Fall of Berlin Campaign, Multiplayer

The Soviet PPSh41 submachine gun was first introduced during the U.S.S.R.'s bitter war with Finland. The PPSh41 utilizes simple blowback action, and fires from the open bolt position. The semi or full auto selector is located within the trigger guard, allowing easy access. A reliable and popular Soviet weapon with a high rate of fire, the PPSh41 used large capacity, cylindrical magazines.

Notes: The PPSh41 is arguably the best submachine gun available. In addition to providing quick, devastating firepower at short and medium range, it also utilizes a 46-round drum magazine. This means you'll have to reload less often. Like the Thompson, the PPSh41 produces a fair amount of recoil, so be ready to compensate for muzzle climb.

Machine Guns

Browning Automatic Rifle

Country of Origin: U.S.

Availability: Multiplayer

Unloaded, the Browning automatic rifle (BAR) is a load. Loaded and ready to fire, it is worth its weight. Use it as a base of fire weapon to cover advancing troops. It has a 20-round clip.

Notes: Although the BAR is fully automatic, it's best to use this function sparingly. The violent recoil makes it difficult to aim while ammo quickly disappears from the limited 20-round clip. When possible, use it to engage enemies at long range with two- to three-round bursts.

27

HISTORICAL NOTES: THE BROWNING AUTOMATIC RIFLE

The initial M1918A1 version of the Browning automatic rifle (BAR) was first used in combat by American soldiers during World War I, and many of these guns saw service in World War II. The BAR received high praise for its reliability under adverse conditions. In 1940, model M1918A2 was adopted.

Unlike earlier models, it could only be fired in two automatic modes—slow (300 to 450 rounds per minute) or fast (500 to 650 rounds per minute)—but not in semiautomatic mode. Both versions were widely used; the BAR was a popular weapon in all theaters because it was reliable and offered an excellent combination of rapid fire and penetrating power. The BAR's only serious drawback was its lack of a quick-change barrel to reduce the chances of overheating.

StG 44 Sturmgewehr

Country of Origin: Germany

Availability: Assault in the Ardennes Campaign, Multiplayer

Tests among German engineers have shown that their standard rifle cartridges are too long and too difficult to target in fully automatic weapons, so the StG 44 Sturmgewehr fires a shorter cartridge. In meeting Hitler's demands for increased production of submachine guns and light machine guns, the StG 44 is considered a resounding achievement of technology and production.

Notes: A precursor to the modern assault rifle, the StG 44 stands out as one of the best weapons available. Its relatively tame recoil, 30-round magazine capacity, and automatic rate of fire make it an extremely versatile weapon that is capable of engaging targets at short or long range. Whenever it's available, make this your primary weapon of choice.

Portable Maschinengewehr 42 (MG-42)

Country of Origin: Germany

Availability:

Multiplayer

Because of its capabilities, the portable MG-42's deadly firepower was widely considered when factoring attacks against the Germans. The MG-42 possessed a very high rate of fire (approximately 1,200 rounds per minute), was extremely reliable in all conditions, was very simple to operate and maintain, and proved to be very popular with the soldiers who called for it in ever-increasing quantities. Quite literally, one man carrying the MG-42 could move with relative freedom with a weapon capable of dominating any infantry battlefield.

Notes: This is primarily a defensive weapon. Because it takes a concentrated effort to tote around and set up, you're not going to charge into enemy fire while carrying it. Instead, place it near an objective already held by your team. When setting it up, make sure your flanks are covered—you don't want enemies sneaking up behind you. Also, try placing it in front of a choke point, but make sure you're not open to fire from enemy snipers.

29

Grenades

Mark II Frag Grenade

Country of Origin: U.S.

Availability: Assault in the Ardennes Campaign, Multiplayer

The lethal range of this hand grenade is 50 yards, so when you throw a Mark II grenade, duck and stay down until it has detonated. Two grenades are standard-issue for each GI.

Notes: The Mark II is a well-rounded frag grenade capable of dispensing shrapnel across a wide area. It also can be thrown quite far, making it a good choice for "cooking." To cook a grenade, hold down the left mouse button for a few seconds before throwing it. If you throw it at the right moment, the grenade will explode in the air, increasing its lethal blast range. However, if you hold the grenade too long, it will explode in your hand. Cooking grenades takes some practice, but it can be a useful tactic once mastered.

HISTORICAL NOTES: THE MARK II FRAG GRENADE

American soldiers used many types of hand grenades during World War II, but the primary hand grenade issued to GIs was the Mark II fragmentation grenade. The Mark II was egg-shaped and constructed of cast iron. The outside of the Mark II was serrated to produce more fragments when it exploded. The specifications for the Mark II called for a TNT filler, but because TNT was in short supply when the war started, many early Mark IIs were filled with a nitrostarch compound.

The time delay on the Mark II's fuse was 4 to 4.8 seconds. The Mark II's killing radius was 5 to 10 yards, but fragments could kill at up to 50 yards. Because the accepted throwing range was 35 to 40 yards, soldiers were ordered to keep their heads down until after the grenade exploded. Of the other types of hand grenades issued to GIs in Europe, the two most common were smoke and phosphorus grenades. Both these grenades were used to mask movements or mark artillery and ground-support aircraft targets.

M36 Mills Bomb

Country of Origin: U.K.

Availability: Operation Overlord Campaign, Multiplayer

The M36 Mills bomb was the standard British hand grenade. The M36 was a cast-iron casing filled with high explosives, utilizing a screw-in fuse that was put in place prior to combat. The fuse itself was activated when a spring-loaded lever was released as the grenade left the thrower's hand. Small, light, and easily thrown a great distance, the M36 surpassed some of its other counterparts in this field, proving to be a deadly weapon in ranged combat.

Notes: The Mills bomb is a great grenade for the open battlefield because of its light weight and impressive range. Try using it against machine gun nests and other enemies utilizing cover.

31

Stielhandgranate

Country of Origin:
Germany

Availability: Assault in
the Ardennes Campaign,
Multiplayer

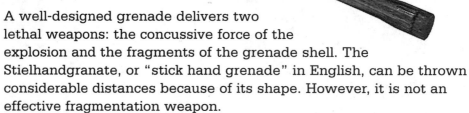

A well-designed grenade delivers two
lethal weapons: the concussive force of the
explosion and the fragments of the grenade shell. The
Stielhandgranate, or "stick hand grenade" in English, can be thrown
considerable distances because of its shape. However, it is not an
effective fragmentation weapon.

Notes: These pipe-shaped grenades are easy to throw long
distances, making them a common threat. Fortunately, they're
relatively easy to see because of their large size and end-over-end
rotation while flying through the air. Sometimes it's best to move
toward an incoming grenade, letting it pass over you, than it is to
move backward in the same direction of its flight path. You also
might catch the thrower without a gun in his hands.

HISTORICAL NOTES: THE STIELHANDGRANATE

As they did with almost every other weapon type, the
Germans developed a number of different hand grenades.
There were, however, two primary types of German high-
explosive hand grenades: the Stielhandgranate 24 ("stick
hand grenade, model 24") and the smaller egg-shaped
Eihandgranate 39 ("egg hand grenade, model 39").

The stick grenade was the better known of the two,
having seen widespread use in World War I and undergoing
various improvements in the interwar years. It consisted of a
thin sheetmetal can containing a TNT charge and was
mounted on a hollow wooden handle. The handle provided
leverage that made this grenade easier to throw than other
egg-shaped German and Allied grenades.

The stick grenade was armed by unscrewing the metal cap on the bottom of the handle to expose a porcelain bead attached to a cord in the handle. Pulling the bead actuated a friction igniter, and the TNT charge exploded after a four- to five-second delay. Late in the war, variant stick grenade models substituted a concrete or wooden charge container for the original metal head.

F1 Fragment Grenade

Country of Origin: U.S.S.R.

Availability: The Fall of Berlin Campaign, Multiplayer

The F1 fragmentation grenade was the Soviet counterpart to the British M36 and the American fragmentation grenades. Heavier than many grenades, the F1 was harder to throw great distances, but it made up for this deficit with its large blast radius.

Notes: The short range and large blast radius make this a dangerous grenade to experiment with. After you throw it, make sure you move (or duck) behind adequate cover—you don't want to watch this one explode. Use the F1 to clear large rooms and other areas where enemies are heavily concentrated.

Smoke Grenades

Smoke grenades are useful in most situations: to obscure the enemy's view, provide cover from enemy fire, or as a diversionary tactic. Although the use of various colors often had meaning, for your European Theater operations the colors have been standardized based on its country.

M18 Smoke Grenade

Country of Origin: U.S.

Availability: Assault in the Ardennes Campaign

Notes: The M18 dispenses red-colored smoke.

RDG-1 Smoke Grenade

Country of Origin: U.S.S.R.

Availability: The Fall of Berlin Campaign

Notes: The RDG-1 dispenses mustard-colored smoke.

Nebelhandgranate

Country of Origin: Germany

Availability: Operation Overlord Campaign

Notes: The Nebelhandgranate dispenses green-colored smoke.

Heavy Weapons

Winchester Shotgun

Country of Origin: U.S.

Availability: Assault in the Ardennes Campaign, Multiplayer

Originally designed as a police weapon, the Winchester shotgun packs a short, solid punch. This solid-framed, pump-action shotgun houses a 20-inch barrel that creates a wide dispersal pattern in the vicinity of the shooter.

Notes: This pump-action shotgun is the ultimate close-quarters weapon. In most cases, you just need to aim in the general direction of an enemy to take him out—as long as he's close enough. Avoid using the shotgun when the range of engagement exceeds more than a few feet. The buckshot disperses as it travels, causing less damage to distant targets. It's a great weapon for clearing rooms.

Bazooka

Country of Origin: U.S.

Availability: Multiplayer

A simple weapon, the bazooka propels a rocket-mounted, three-pound grenade in the direction the tube is pointed. Early models required two soldiers to operate, one to fire and one to load. And, they were often dangerous. However, design flaws have been eliminated, and the bazooka has become an effective field weapon.

Notes: Although useful as an anti-tank weapon, the bazooka is also an effective weapon against enemy personnel. While it's equipped, you'll move very slowly. Switch to your pistol to move faster, then raise the bazooka once you're ready to fire.

35

HISTORICAL NOTES: THE BAZOOKA

In response to the need for an infantry anti-tank weapon, Leslie A. Skinner and Edward G. Uhl of the Ordnance Department developed the bazooka—a metal tube that used an electrical firing mechanism—by early 1942. Until then, American infantry had lacked an anti-tank rocket capable of stopping a tank.

Another member of the Ordnance Department, Henry H. Mohaupt, had been working on a shaped-charge grenade for use by infantry against tanks. Mohaupt's M10 grenade weighed over 3.5 pounds, making it nearly impossible to throw effectively. However, when Skinner and Uhl started attaching Mohaupt's grenades to their bazooka rocket, scoring hits on three successive shots during testing, the Ordnance Department immediately recognized the value of this new weapon.

Many bazookas were shipped to America's allies; in fact, when the Germans captured one, they copied the design to produce the Panzerschreck ("tank terror"). The bazooka was named for a musical contraption devised by comedian Bob Burns.

Gewehrgrante

Country of Origin: Germany

Availability: Multiplayer

The Gewehrgrante is mounted beneath the barrel of a standard issue KAR 98K and capable of launching the Mod.30 High Explosive (HE) Rifle Grenade. The innovative rifling design of the 30mm grenade provides increased accuracy and range over earlier rifle grenades. This design also facilitates the use of a larger warhead, making it an equally dangerous threat to both personnel and light vehicles.

Notes: When using the Gewehrgrante, make sure your allies are clear of the impact area. Like regular hand grenades, this weapon is capable of delivering a tremendous amount of damage over great distances. For best effect, use it in the opening moments of an assault when the enemy is still at long range.

36

Panzerschreck

Country of Origin: Germany

Availability: Assault in the Ardennes Campaign, Multiplayer

The larger cousin of the grenade-launching Panzerfaust, the Panzerschreck propels a rocket-powered grenade from a shoulder-held tube. A rough shield with a small opening for aiming provides the operator with some protection from the exhaust blast of the rocket.

Notes: The Panzerschreck is nearly identical to the bazooka. You'll mainly use it against enemy armor, but it can be fired at infantry, too. The reload time is extremely slow, so make sure you have a new round loaded before stowing it—you won't want to take the time to reload it if an enemy tank surprises you around the next corner. Panzerschreck rounds travel slowly, making it tough to hit moving targets, but this works in your favor when you're on the receiving end.

Mountable Weapons

MG-42

Country of Origin: Germany

Availability:
All Campaigns, Multiplayer

A unique delayed-blowback firing system allows the gun to achieve rates of fire three times greater than any American machine gun. MG-42s are used extensively in cover and defensive situations throughout the European theater.

37

Notes: The MG-42 can lay down a wall of lead in a matter of seconds, making it great for engaging multiple enemies. However, it has a limited firing arc, leaving it open to flanking maneuvers. So when you're not firing it, back off and check your perimeter.

AA Gun

Country of Origin: Germany

Availability: Assault in the Ardennes Campaign, Operation Overlord Campaign, Multiplayer

Notes: The AA Gun is a bulky piece of machinery with four barrels capable of automatic fire. It takes a few seconds for the gun to warm up once the trigger is pulled. Designed as an anti-aircraft weapon, also use it to engage ground targets. With enough concentrated hits, it has enough firepower to destroy a tank.

Nebelwerfer

Country of Origin: Germany

Availability: Assault in the Ardennes Campaign, Multiplayer

Notes: The Nebelwerfer is a six-barrel artillery piece that fires explosive rocket rounds. It can fire six rockets in quick succession, but there's a lengthy reload process. When firing at infantry, aim for their feet— the splash damage from the explosion will take them out.

Soviet 7.62mm DTM

Country of Origin: U.S.S.R.

Availability: The Fall of Berlin Campaign

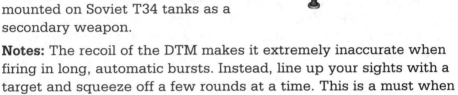

It has a 60-round, detachable pan capacity and violent firing recoil. The DTM was rarely used as a stand-alone weapon. Cumbersome and large, these weapons gained popularity when mounted on Soviet T34 tanks as a secondary weapon.

Notes: The recoil of the DTM makes it extremely inaccurate when firing in long, automatic bursts. Instead, line up your sights with a target and squeeze off a few rounds at a time. This is a must when engaging infantry at long (or even medium) range.

88mm Flak Cannon

Country of Origin: Germany

Availability: All Campaigns, Multiplayer

Notes: Like the AA gun, the flak cannon was originally designed as an anti-aircraft gun. But its large 88mm proved to be effective for taking out tanks also. Firing is as simple as lining up the crosshairs and pulling the trigger. Be prepared for a lengthy reloading process between shots.

39

PzB41

Country of Origin: Germany

Availability: Assault in the Ardennes Campaign

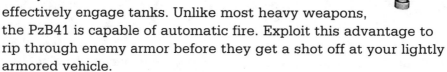

Notes: A PzB41 mounted on a halftrack gives it the ability to effectively engage tanks. Unlike most heavy weapons, the PzB41 is capable of automatic fire. Exploit this advantage to rip through enemy armor before they get a shot off at your lightly armored vehicle.

Granatwerfer

Country of Origin: Germany

Availability: Assault in the Ardennes Campaign, The Fall of Berlin Campaign, Multiplayer

Notes: This is one of the trickiest weapons at your disposal, but with some practice you should be able to place mortar rounds with precision. Use the mouse to rotate and adjust the pitch of the mortar tube. Lowering the pitch increases the mortar's range and raising it decreases the range. Experiment with a couple of shots before you hit your intended target. The mortar is a very deadly weapon, so make sure you're not firing on allies. It's best used in situations where you can place rounds on narrow choke points, such as alleys and other predictable thoroughfares.

Items and Equipment

Binoculars

The binoculars are an important tactical device, allowing you to scout ahead before moving in a particular direction. Sometimes they'll reveal enemies lying in wait that you wouldn't be able to see otherwise. The binoculars also can help you target enemies when you don't have a sniper rifle. Line up

the target in the center of the binoculars and, without moving the mouse, switch back to a rifle—you should be lined up with the target. Fire a few shots, then switch back to the binocular view to inspect the target. If you lined up things properly to begin with, your target should be on the ground.

Explosive Charge

Place these timed explosives on objectives slated for demolition. Whenever an object can be destroyed with an explosive, a transparent red box (in the shape of a charge) appears somewhere on the target. Once you find this spot, press E to place the charge. This initiates a timer countdown to detonation. Move away before it explodes.

41

Sticky Bomb

Sticky bombs perform the same function as explosive charges, but lack the fancy technology of a timing device. Instead, these satchels of explosives have a fuse that must be lit. Rain will extinguish these fuses, requiring you to shoot the bomb from a safe distance to trigger detonation. Look for the plume of white smoke to spot the smoldering fuse.

Ammunition

To complete your missions, you need to retrieve ammo from the battlefield. The most common way to do this is to pick up ammo from dropped weapons. On occasion, you may find boxes of ammo, providing a quick boost to your inventory. Either way, keep track of your ammo count for each weapon type and concentrate on using the weapon with the most ammo available.

NOTE

With the exception of heavy weapons, ammo is interchangeable within classes. For example, SMG ammo taken from an MP-40 will work in all submachine guns.

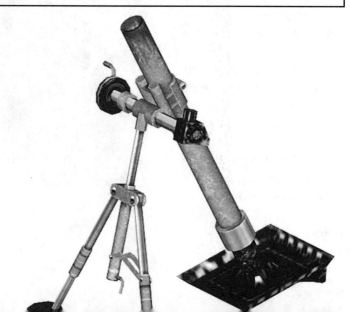

Medical Supplies

In addition to ammo, you also need to seek out medical supplies to replenish your health meter. There are four types of supplies available.

Medicinal Canteen

Restores 25% of your total health

The medicinal canteen is the most common form of medical aid. They're usually dropped by enemy soldiers and can be gathered after a firefight along with ammo.

First Aid Kit

Restores 50% of your total health

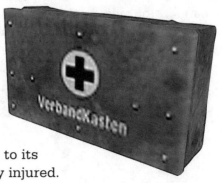

First aid kits aren't as common as medicinal canteens. They're usually retrieved from specific locations and aren't carried around by enemy soldiers. Check behind machine gun nests and on tables inside buildings.

Field Surgeon Pack

Restores 100% of your total health

Field surgeon packs are quite rare, appearing in a few specific places and situations. You'll rarely need the full attention it provides, so consider moving forward and backtracking to its location when you're substantially injured.

Health Barrel

Restores 100% of your tank's total health

When driving the T34, you'll want to pick up these health barrels to repair your tank. Try to go without picking one up until you're desperate—there are only a few and you'll want to clear as much of the city as possible.

Vehicles

C-47 Skytrain

Country of Origin: U.S.

The C-47 Skytrain is a workhorse of a transport plane, carrying a 7,500-pound payload at an operational ceiling of 24,000 feet. Other roles include reconnaissance, evacuation, glider towing, psychological warfare, and even battle when outfitted with guns.

Notes: C-47s serve a critical role in the pre-dawn invasion at Normandy. Not only do they drop paratroopers, but they also airdrop supplies needed to complete crucial mission objectives.

L-4 Piper Cub

Country of Origin: U.S.

First introduced in 1937, the unarmed Piper Cub found immediate favor with the military as a training vehicle for pilots. Subsequent versions now feature larger engines, up to 65 horsepower, which can carry its all-metal fuselage at higher speeds. The U.S. Army has put the plane into action as an observation platform, VIP transport, and spotter.

Notes: You'll need to find one of these downed reconnaissance airplanes during the attack on Berlin.

T34

Country of Origin: U.S.S.R.

Notes: Driving tanks is a bit different than regular movement. The chassis moves independently of the turret's facing. While driving the T34, alternate between the DTM and the main gun. The main gun takes a while to load between shots, so make the most of the time by firing at enemy troops with the machine gun.

45

Opel Blitz Three-Ton Truck

Country of Origin: Germany

This rear-wheel drive truck serves many functions. Any of several bodies can be slapped onto the chassis, whose rugged design can accommodate its different chores. A 3.6-liter engine delivers 68 horses through five forward speeds.

Notes: Trucks often carry reinforcements to the battlefield. If possible, destroy them while enemy troops are still inside. Do this by targeting them with mounted weapons like AA guns or flak cannons. In some situations, you can use sticky bombs to destroy them. You can also use multiple grenades to destroy trucks, but it's best to save them for other situations.

BMW R75M Motorcycle with Sidecar

Country of Origin: Germany

By adding a sidecar to this BMW design, a gunner can be carried along to protect the driver and any other cargo on roads or across rough terrain.

Notes: You won't have to worry about engaging any of these motorcycles in the campaigns. They only make a couple of brief (but memorable) cameo appearances. For instance, this is how the Colonel makes his escape.

Sd. Kfz. 251 Armored Halftrack

Country of Origin: Germany

An armored hull sits on top of a three-ton chassis that can carry troops at speeds that keep pace with tank units. Among the 22 variants of the 251 are flamethrowers, anti-tank versions, communications hubs, and rocket launchers. Most are equipped with an MG-34 machine gun, at least.

Notes: Although armored, halftracks have an exposed top that allows you to shoot down inside them—that is if you're firing from an elevated position. If you have a good arm, you can even toss a grenade inside them. This probably won't destroy the halftrack, but it's a good way to take out any passengers.

Panzerwerfer

Country of Origin: Germany

Notes: The Panzerwerfer is a modified halftrack that carries rockets. You'll come across a few of these during your escape from Berlin. The rockets do about the same damage as a Panzerschreck round, so make these vehicles a priority whenever they come into view.

47

Pz. Kpfw. VI Tiger

Country of Origin: Germany

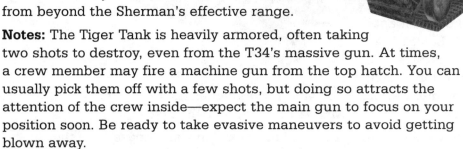

Despite regular mechanical problems and a low top-speed, the Tiger carries the most effective gun of the war, the 88mm cannon. It is very well-armored and can destroy Sherman tanks from beyond the Sherman's effective range.

Notes: The Tiger Tank is heavily armored, often taking two shots to destroy, even from the T34's massive gun. At times, a crew member may fire a machine gun from the top hatch. You can usually pick them off with a few shots, but doing so attracts the attention of the crew inside—expect the main gun to focus on your position soon. Be ready to take evasive maneuvers to avoid getting blown away.

Pz. Kpfw. IV Medium Tank

Country of Origin: Germany

The basic tank chassis of the Pz. Kpfw. IV has spawned a number of derivatives, including a tank destroyer assault gun, a self-propelled 88mm howitzer, and varieties of anti-tank aircraft that use mounted 20mm quad guns against airborne targets.

Notes: When on foot, you'll need to use sticky bombs to take out these tanks. But before running up and slapping one on, look for any soldiers riding on top. Even after the tank is destroyed, watch for surviving crew members climbing out. Although tank crews will initially try to get away, they may regroup and counterattack. Don't let this happen.

Junkers JU-87 Stuka

Country of Origin: Germany

Although effective, the JU-87 requires air superiority before it can attack. When it begins a dive bomb run, it's very vulnerable to interception from above.

Notes: The only way to take out these bombers is to shoot them down with an AA gun. Open fire just ahead of them, forcing them to fly through your rapid fire. It'll take several passes before they spiral out of control.

49

3
OPERATION OVERLORD

The Hour Is Go

—Francis J. Turner, from his personal archives

One's eyes close tight and families fade,
When going to war which evil men made.
Though anxious and frightened, we don't let it show,
For the day is approaching, when the Airborne must go.

Each day now rolls past; we wait just the same,
But D-Day is near, and for this we all came.
The hour grows near; each man feels it inside,
And soon we'll be falling, with nowhere to hide.

Our eyes are now down and the chatter the same,
Each weapon now loaded, no longer a game.
Eagles gather round and bow your heads low,
Europe awaits and the hour is go.

Planes rumble past as we wait for our turn,
To fly over waters we have yet to each earn.
Checked buckles and straps, left nothing to chance,
The Jumpmaster stands, calls "Welcome to France."

Flak turns to fire in the blackest of night,
Too low, too fast, can't jump from this height.
There's no turning back, the risk has been taken,
Free fall into hell, paratrooper's forsaken.

Eagles hold tight, scattered prayers to survive,
We'll hit the ground soon, whether dead or alive.
As feet touch the ground, each soldier turns on,
Confusion and fear are beaten and gone.

The enemy is close and sad they don't know
The Airborne is here, it's time they must go.
The hour is now, Hitler's had his last chance
On St. Michael's wings, we're taking back France.

51

Welcome to France

June 6, 1944

Normandy, France

D-Day

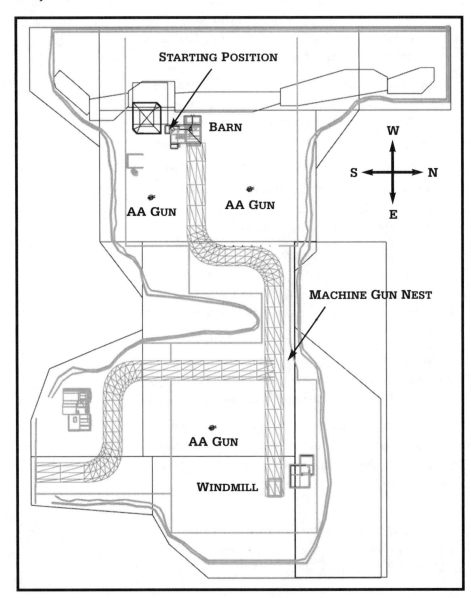

After parachuting in five miles inland from Omaha Beach with the British 6th Airborne Division, you set out on a top-secret mission to destroy German fortified artillery positions. In hours, Allied forces will begin the D-Day invasion. Your success or failure in knocking out these installations will have an impact on what happens when the troops land on the beach.

Take a good look around. You probably won't see these guys again.

You begin the mission in a cramped C-47 cruising at 3,000 feet. As you approach the drop zone, the green light signals the time to jump. The anti-aircraft (AA) gun tracer rounds illuminating the night sky indicate the enemy's heightened state of alert. Your situation is further complicated when you parachute through a barn's roof. So much for a surprise attack.

INITIAL OBJECTIVE

• Rendezvous with Allies

Press the use key (default E) to free yourself of the parachute harness. After you hit the ground, back step into the small square room and pull out your M1. The two soldiers in the barn (one on the ground level, and one in the loft) spot you—be ready for them. If you can't see them, side step until you can get a clear shot.

Take out the soldier on the upper level first—he's the one who'll throw grenades into your hiding spot. Be careful, though, you're at close range. Your marksmanship may be off, but theirs won't be. Drop them before they can shoot.

While floating down, make a mental note of certain landmarks—particularly the position of the two AA guns.

From the barn's loft, use the M1 to take out the two soldiers on the stream's other side.

After dispatching the two soldiers in the barn, approach the window ahead with the large haystacks next to it. Do not expose yourself—there's a soldier with an MP-40 on the other side. Move to the window's right and side step left to take him out. When he's down, backtrack to the stairs heading to the loft. Stay along the right side of the steps as you go up—the left side is broken.

TIP
There's a first aid kit on the table inside the barn.

With the M1 in hand, move to the left at the top of the stairs toward the opening. There are two soldiers on the other side of the small stream. They are hard to see in the darkness, but their muzzle flashes give them away. Crouch to make yourself a smaller target and open up with the M1 until both are down.

Stay to the right of the loft's opening until you take out the first soldier. Step to the left until you can see the other one. Watch their bodies to make sure they're dead. The M1 is powerful enough to knock them down, but sometimes the bullets will pass through without neutralizing them.

When the coast is clear, jump out of the loft into the small stream below. You land next to a soldier who's face down in the water— his chute failed. He has nothing on him you can use. Face east while strafing to the left to hit a few soldiers on the bank above. One tosses a grenade into the stream, so get out and take them down. When the shooting stops, gather ammo and an MP-40 off their bodies.

Side step left until you can climb out of the streambed.

TIP

Use a frag grenade to clear the soldiers on the bank above. The Colt .45 is good for engaging survivors at close range when you're rushing out of the stream.

55

Turn your attention to the AA gun to the east. As you inch forward, a couple of soldiers fires on you. Take them down —you need to make it to that gun. There's a third soldier hiding on the opposite side of the gun. Use the MP-40 to mow him down as you run forward. A truck full of reinforcements is coming down the road from the east. Destroy it before the troops can get out. The AA gun takes time to warm up, so don't worry about opening fire before adjusting your aim. After the truck is smoldering, listen for shots coming from the field to the south. Fire a few rounds in the direction of any muzzle flashes.

A few well-placed rounds with the AA gun are enough to leave this truck in flames.

> ### TIP
> Take out the truck so it doesn't block your view of the AA gun in the opposite field. This allows you to aim at any soldiers on the other side. There is a medicinal canteen in the back of the truck.

Approach the field to the south. If you did your job right, the other field is quiet. If not, crouch and use the trees lining the road for cover. The soldiers will see you before you see them, so listen and watch for automatic gunfire. Place an obstacle between you and them. Fortunately, they won't be accurate at this range, but you still need cover. Side step in and out of cover to exchange shots until any opposition is down.

56

From the field containing the second AA gun, move east, toward the fenceline. As you move forward, three soldiers appear down the road. One takes a position among the trees to the right, while the other two will drop on the road and open fire. Backtrack to the AA gun and use it for cover. You can't rotate the gun in their direction. Instead, hide behind it and pick off each soldier with

Use the AA gun in the southern field for cover while you dispatch the three soldiers down the road.

the M1. It may take several attempts to drop the soldiers from this range, but be persistent and adjust your aim with each missed shot. When you think they're down, move forward, listening for shots. Pick up some ammo and a medicinal canteen.

Use the binoculars to spot this machine gun nest.

While you're collecting gear, two soldiers approach from the north. Take cover behind some trees and drop them with the M1. They'll drop SMG ammo and a medicinal canteen. But don't gather their gear yet. Along the left side of the road to the north, there's a machine gun nest waiting for you to move forward. Crouch and inch forward while staying behind the trees on the right side of the road. Use the binoculars to spot a row of sandbags—the machine gunner is on the other side. You can't get in range for a grenade toss, so you'll have to eliminate the gunner with some clever marksmanship. While taking cover behind the trees, slowly move forward until you reach the base of the sandbags. Stand up,

57

then duck. If the machine gun opens fire, it means the gunner can see you—but you can see him, too. Using the trees for cover, stand and duck a few times until you can get a fix on the gunner's position—he's situated in the middle. With your M1 equipped, aim above the muzzle flashes and fire a shot. Do this until the opposing fire halts. Before moving forward, use the binoculars again to verify the gunner is down.

With the machine gun silent, move toward it. Behind the sandbags is SMG ammo and a first aid kit. But don't pick them up yet. A patrol of five enemy soldiers is moving toward you from the direction you came. Use the MG-42 to mow them down. They leave behind assorted ammo and a medicinal canteen.

Use the MG-42 to mow down the patrol approaching from the west.

> **TIP**
> Your crosshairs turn green when placed over friendly targets—don't shoot them.

As you continue down the road to the east, you'll see the silhouette of a windmill, where a gun battle is taking place. A few sadistic soldiers are taking shots at a paratrooper hanging from one of the windmill's blades. Move forward, but watch your fire—there are friendlies in the area. As you get closer, a red smoke grenade arcs across the sky from behind the windmill. Help the outnumbered three-man squad of British paratroopers assault the four enemy soldiers. When it's clear, approach the British squad to complete your first objective.

58

Destroying the Tank

NEW OBJECTIVES

- Destroy tank with AA gun
- Regroup with Allies

A German tank breaks through and poses a threat to you and your new friends. Run toward the AA gun southeast of the windmill and open fire on the tank. It won't take long before it's reduced to a flaming hulk. Return to your squad, grab your gear, and follow the Captain out of the area.

Your squadmates draw the tank's fire while you pound at it with the AA gun.

The Causeway

Your next mission arrives via radio transmission: Destroy a key enemy-held bridge and eliminate the German colonel in charge of defending it. After recovering from the jump, move forward. By destroying the bridge, you'll cripple the enemy's ability to transport heavy artillery by train to the Normandy coast. Before blowing up the bridge, you must first cross the river to locate the Nazi Colonel.

NEW OBJECTIVE

- Locate and destroy two artillery emplacements

Your primary task for this mission is to take out two 88s shelling Omaha Beach. Omaha Beach is a primary landing spot for the amphibious portion of the Allied invasion, which is scheduled to begin in a few hours. Once you silence the artillery, continue onto the bridge. When the Captain has received the orders, he commands you to take point.

59

The Causeway

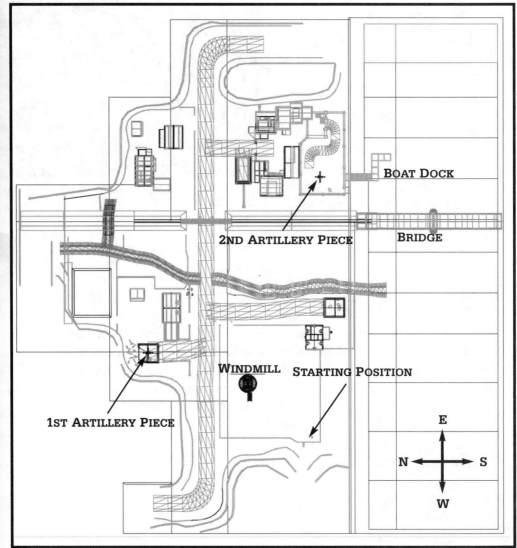

BOAT DOCK

2ND ARTILLERY PIECE

BRIDGE

WINDMILL   STARTING POSITION

1ST ARTILLERY PIECE

E

N   S

W

Lead the squad to the large, southwest windmill. Equip the Sten Mark 2 submachine gun and approach the staircase leading to the upper level of the windmill—there's a German sniper hiding inside. Watch the two soldiers in the lower portion of the windmill. One comes out and opens fire on your squad—take him out. Enter the lower room to neutralize the second soldier. Pick up the medicinal canteen. Exit the lower room and move back to the stairs.

At the top of the stairs, open the door and quickly shoot the sniper. When he falls, approach the window overlooking the east road and spot a couple of soldiers —time for some sniping of your own. Equip the Lee Enfield and shoot the soldiers. Move to the north window. Draw fire from the area just in front of the garage. Use the muzzle flashes to line up your shots, and open fire with the Enfield. There

Be sure to get the second solider in the windmill's lower level.

should be about three soldiers in that particular area. Use the binoculars to get a better idea of where they're hiding. Eliminating the sniper and other soldiers now makes things easier and safer as you continue with your mission.

Return to your squad and head toward the small, eastern farmhouse. This little house (and the accompanying garage) is swarming with German troops; shoot them fast, before they get a chance to fortify their positions. As you approach the house, a soldier exits through the front door and moves toward you. Help your squad mow him down. Watch and listen for more activity inside.

61

When activity slows down, slowly approach the eastern face of the house, keeping clear of the windows on the front side—there are still some enemy troops inside, so make sure you have a full clip—it's time for some close-quarters combat. While crouching, slowly edge around the front of the house and pause for a few seconds. Some soldiers may come running out of the house. Mow them down.

Fire through the windows to take out the soldiers inside.

Stand up and slowly side step to peek through the first window until you can see any enemy soldiers lying in wait. Your squadmates help you dispatch any enemies by firing through the windows.

Once it looks clear, take the lead (with the Sten still in hand) and sweep each room of the small house. Stay clear of the back door (leading out onto the enclosed porch) until the rest of the house is clear. Make sure your squad is with you before heading for the garage.

As you exit the main part of the house into the back porch, face the wooden garage to the west. Troops positioned in front of the garage immediately begin to fire into the porch's windows—this isn't a good place to stay. Quickly run out of the porch and along the eastern wall of the garage while firing the Sten. Your squadmates will engage the enemy from the back porch while you flank the enemy. Slowly move toward the front of the garage while taking out any enemies that get in your way. Pause near the open garage doors and wait for more Germans to run out.

Once things slow down, side step around the small open door and peek inside. Be ready to open fire on any soldiers you might find hiding behind the crates. The panicked troops inside will begin firing even if they can't see you. If possible, let them expend a clip of ammunition before storming the garage. Pay attention to their firing patterns and listen for a pause and the telltale clicks of changing magazines. Use this opportunity to rush in and take them down. If you miss, find cover behind a crate and crouch down. Chances are, any remaining troops will be hiding behind crates as well, so search each concealed portion of the garage before letting your guard down. When things are clear, check out the garage for some SMG ammo, a medicinal canteen, and a box of grenades.

> **TIP**
> Press E to pick up the box of grenades.

With the farmhouse and garage clear, pull out the Enfield and head down the road leading south. Hug the eastern fenceline as you move along the road. About halfway down the road, a couple soldiers open fire at the end of the road. Drop them before moving forward.

Watch out for soldiers hiding behind crates in the garage.

Quickly get to the end of the road and take cover in an impact crater on the left side of the intersection. About this time (if not before), you'll come under fire from troops guarding the first 88mm gun in front of another garage to the southeast. The resistance may be smaller if you took out some of them at the windmill. You'll also hear the 88mm gun at work. Crouch down in the crater for cover and watch for muzzle flashes. Even if you can't make out clear shots just yet, begin firing in their general direction to keep them from advancing. With the help of your squad, fire on the enemy troops as they become visible and wait for a lull in the gunfire before leaving the crater.

Next, quickly move across the road toward the white house to the south. Press up against the house's northern face and move west until you're up against the small stone wall. Hold this position and wait for more troops to charge down the driveway from the south.

63

As they run past you, surprise them with a few quick barks from your Sten. A couple soldiers on the opposite side of the driveway begin exchanging fire while ducking behind a stone wall of their own. Watch for them to pop up, and pick them off. If you expend a clip during this gun battle, crouch down and use the wall for protection while reloading.

Ambush the soldiers moving from the south while hiding behind this stone wall.

> **TIP**
>
> While hiding behind the stone wall, watch out for incoming grenades thrown from the other side of the driveway.

When it looks clear, jump up onto the stone wall and slowly inch to your left around the corner of the house while facing the garage to the north. Take out the two guards in front of the garage and pursue them if they try to retreat. Once they're dispatched, the Captain and the rest of the squad will move forward for the assault on the garage.

Don't worry about opening the door. One of your squadmates will blow away the small door to the left with a hand grenade—so stand back. When the door is gone, help your squad mop up any troops hiding inside. As in the previous garage assault, engage as many enemies as you can from the doorway and watch out for guards hiding behind crates. Once you have a good idea of where the enemies are positioned, enter to clean house. After you've eliminated the guards, the Captain tells you to place a charge on the artillery piece, then join the rest of the squad outside. Before setting the charge, scour the room for some ammo, a medicinal canteen, and a first aid kit.

Look for the transparent red charge icon flashing on the gun's south facing leg. Approach the spot and press Ⓔ to place the charge. The timer is pretty short, so quickly exit the garage and immediately turn right to join your squad taking cover behind the stone wall.

After the charge explodes, a group of late reinforcements will approach from the opposite side of the garage. Stay behind the stone wall and engage them with the Sten as they pop around the corner. If you let them get too close, they'll move into the garage for cover. Prevent them from taking up positions in the garage—it can be difficult to ferret them out, plus they can flank your position from inside. As the gunfire

The explosive charge destroys the first gun but attracts reinforcements—be ready!

ceases, cautiously move around the western side of the garage and peek around the corner. Take out any troops that may be lying in wait there.

> ### TIP
> **Pick up a couple of medicinal canteens in the single-story structure connected to the barn.**

Now move through the field to the northeast until you come to a grate situated below some train tracks. The Captain orders Private Galloway to destroy the grate with explosives. Stand back until it explodes, then move through the short tunnel. On the other side,

turn right and follow
Galloway behind the barn.
Take out the soldier
standing in the barn's loft
and continue forward. About
this time, Private Galloway
will get hit from fire coming
within the barn. Follow the
Captain's orders and circle
around the eastern side of
the structure.

Take out this soldier hiding in the barn's loft before
he notices you.

TIP

**Private Galloway's death is
scripted and can't be prevented.**

Use the Sten to gun down
any soldiers exiting through
the barn doors. Enter
the barn to clear out any
survivors—there are usually
two or three soldiers hiding
in the haystacks.

Climb to the upper level
of the barn and approach
the eastern opening
overlooking the back of the
house. A few soldiers will
move around the far side of
the house. Surprise them

Aim at the barn doors and shoot anything that comes out.

with some well-placed shots from the Enfield. Your squadmates will
engage them from the ground, catching them in a crossfire. Once the
shooting stops, drop to the ground and move around the far east
corner of the house. Take out any soldiers hiding here and continue
south, across the road, to an iron gate.

Stop to the right side of the gate and wait for the Captain to open it. Hold this position and provide cover fire while your two squadmates move to one of the buildings on the left. Use the Sten to take down as many threats as possible. There are two soldiers in the second floor windows just opposite the gate. There are also a couple soldiers in the wooden shed to the west.

Take this position at the iron gate to provide covering fire for your squadmates.

Take out the four soldiers to eliminate the enemy's crossfire advantage. Next, concentrate your fire on the buildings to the east.

Once things cool down a bit, cross the courtyard to help your squadmates assault the far southeast building. Clear out the bottom floor and then aim up at the stairway and wait for more soldiers to move into your sights. Follow your squadmates to the second floor and help mop up any resistance.

From the upper floor, you can see the second 88mm gun to the west. Wait for the Captain's signal before assaulting it.

From the upper floor, you can see the second 88 firing in the distance. The Captain orders you to take it out while he provides cover fire. Move out onto the balcony and follow the steps down, moving west toward the gun. As you approach the rocks to the right, the Captain opens fire. Join in and mow down any soldiers that come into your sights.

Cautiously approach the gun. There may be some more soldiers lurking around the tent. Once the area is clear, place a charge on the gun and move away.

After the gun is destroyed, the Captain joins you. Private Wilson also returns to report he's found a way across the river. Gather the ammo and medicinal canteens scattered around the destroyed gun and follow your squadmates to a dock where a rowboat is waiting.

TIP

When assaulting the last 88, wait for the Captain to open fire first. If you attack prematurely, the crew will turn the gun around at the building and kill the Captain. This results in a mission failure.

A Train To Catch

After crossing the river, you and the remaining members of your squad must hunt down the evasive Colonel. Searching from house to house, don't stop until you find him and carry out one of your prime mission objectives—his assassination. When moving on to the bridge, be resourceful, using German artillery and locating air-dropped supplies. You'll need all the firepower you can muster when facing German armor. Rely on all of your training to blow the bridge before a train loaded with heavy artillery arrives at the station.

Plant a charge on the last artillery piece to complete your objectives.

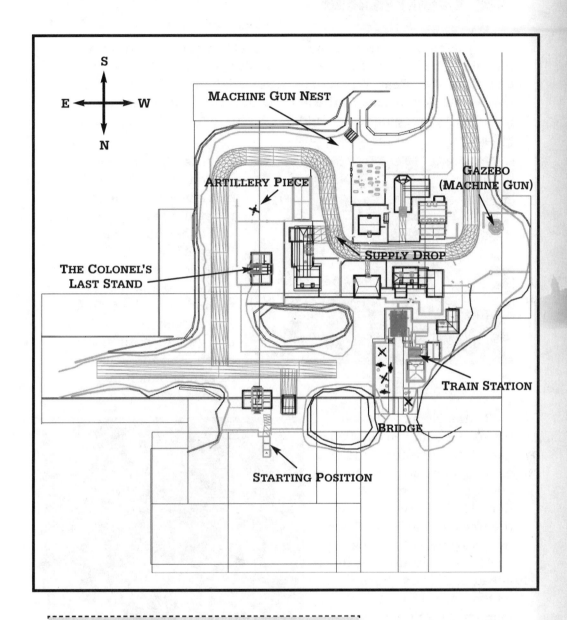

MACHINE GUN NEST

GAZEBO (MACHINE GUN)

ARTILLERY PIECE

SUPPLY DROP

THE COLONEL'S LAST STAND

TRAIN STATION

BRIDGE

STARTING POSITION

S
E — W
N

NEW OBJECTIVES

- Accompany your squad across the river
- Track and eliminate the colonel

69

As you cross the river, equip the Enfield. A couple soldiers are patrolling the bank of the river, but don't open fire—they don't pose an immediate threat. When the boat reaches the dock, jump out and follow your squad toward the large house. Help them shoot any soldiers that appear. You should be able to take out three or four without even entering the house.

Take out as many soldiers as possible from the front of the house before moving inside.

When things cool off, switch to the Sten and move inside. Clear each room and make your way to the back of the house. Stop before going out the back door and wait for two soldiers to approach. Gun them down. The Colonel zooms past on a motorcycle and down a road to the south. Exit the house and clear any remaining opposition outside.

Cautiously move toward the road leading south. Pause near the intersection and engage a few soldiers moving down the road with the Enfield. Take cover behind the trees on the right. Once the two patrolling soldiers are down, concentrate your fire ahead at the next house on the right. The Colonel's motorcycle is parked out front, and if you get close enough, you see him taking shots at you with his pistol. As you move closer, the Colonel runs inside the house to the right.

The Colonel narrowly escapes on a motorcycle. Follow him!

Before chasing down the Colonel, take out several soldiers in and around the house. Move toward the front of the house and wait for a few soldiers to come around the far corner of the house. Help your squad take them out. Watch out for a soldier crouched beneath the low wall surrounding the front of the house. He may toss grenades at you. Either throw a grenade at his position or gun him down as he stands up.

Approach the front door, but don't enter just yet. The Colonel is standing at the top of the stairs, firing at you. Return fire and wait for him to retreat. A few more soldiers will approach from one of the rooms to the left. Use the Sten to gun them down. Circle around the ground floor and eliminate any more soldiers before going after the Colonel.

Clear out the bottom floor before going after the Colonel.

Once it's clear, climb the stairs and head down the adjoining hallway until you can see the Colonel standing on the balcony. Center the crosshairs on his torso and fire until he falls over the railing.

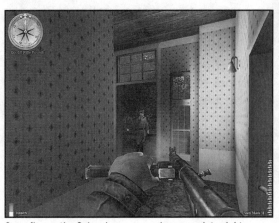

Open fire on the Colonel as soon as he comes into sight.

TIP

Although he's only equipped with a pistol, the Colonel is extremely accurate and dangerous. Take him down quickly with a long burst from the Sten.

71

Return to front of the house to rejoin your squad. Follow them down the road to the south. Suddenly a Tiger Tank breaks through a stone wall to the right. Before your squad can take cover, it fires its main gun, killing Private Wilson.

Tank Ambush

NEW OBJECTIVE

- Destroy the Tiger Tank with the flak cannon
- Use a demolition charge to destroy the flak cannon

The Captain orders you to man the nearby 88mm gun while he draws the tank within your range. Move through the broken wall to your right and spot the unoccupied 88mm gun. Move behind it and press E to activate it. Don't bother shooting out the walls ahead—the Tiger Tank will take care of that for you.

Be patient and make your shots count. It only takes two direct hits to knock out the Tiger Tank.

Wait until the Tank comes into view and fire the first round at its left side. This gets the tank's attention. Patiently wait for the next shell to load and fire again. It's enough to destroy the tank.

Once the tank is rubble, the Captain orders you to place a charge on the 88. Place the charge at the base of the gun and move toward the Captain. About this time a C-47 flies over, and drops your supplies (explosives to take out the bridge) on a road to the west.

The Supplies

NEW OBJECTIVE

• Acquire explosives from the air drop

Turn down the western road and take position behind the burned-out tank. A couple of soldiers across the road take cover behind the stone wall in front of the church. Use the Enfield to take them out. Switch back to the Sten and mow down the four soldiers who come around the northern wall. Once they're down, turn your attention to the machine gun nest just on the other side of the truck to your left.

This is a good spot to ambush the four incoming soldiers who round the corner.

This machine gun covers the road running to the north—the same road your supplies are sitting on. You'll have to take out the gunner. Using the broken-down truck for cover, equip a smoke grenade and throw it to the other side of the truck. Wait a few seconds for the smoke to disperse, then peek around the truck. If the gunner's view is obscured, he won't shoot. However, you won't be able to see the gunner, either.

While the smoke is still effective, rush forward with the Sten equipped and take out the gunner before he sees you approach. The best way to do this is to move around the front of the truck and along the far right side of the gunner's position. Even if he sees you, he won't be able to rotate the machine gun in your direction. But he still has an MP-40, which can be just as dangerous at this range. Drop him before he has a chance to use it.

73

Now move toward the supplies. Once the machine gunner is neutralized, the Captain takes a position along the right side of the road running north. Stay to the left and help the Captain take out the German troops ahead. Move slowly, using cover when available. The large boulder on the left side of the road is a nice spot— just watch out for incoming grenades. Ignore the supplies in the middle of the road until the opposition drops off.

Use a smoke grenade to obscure the machine gunner's view. Then rush in to flank his position.

Take out the two soldiers on the other side of the barb wire down the western road. Once everything is clear, approach the supplies and take the explosives. Now you're ready to go after the bridge.

TIP

The firefight near the supply drop can get really heated. Keep an eye on the Captain and make sure he's not getting hit too badly. If he dies, the mission is over. Consider using the Enfield to knock down the enemy soldiers from a distance. Then switch to the Sten as the action gets closer.

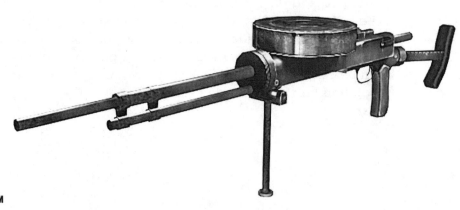

On to the Bridge

NEW OBJECTIVE

• Plant four demolition charges on the bridge

From the point where you picked up the explosives, turn west and enter the gate. Follow the path around the building to the left, but watch out for three enemy soldiers. Be prepared to drop them with the Sten. Once it's clear, continue along the path until you come to a small wooden communications shack. Place a charge next to the radio and stand back. The explosion will rip a hole in the back wall, allowing you to pass into a courtyard in front of the church. As you move through the opening, a soldier appears straight ahead. Shoot him.

The courtyard has high stone walls, providing good cover while allowing you to see the heads of enemies on the other side. Use this opportunity to pick off a few soldiers.

Use one of the charges to blow a hole in the back of this communications shack.

TIP

Stay on the southern side of the church courtyard. If you move too far north, a machine gunner in a gazebo at the end of the road fires at you from the west. You'll get to him soon enough.

Next, continue west toward the green building, and turn down the alley to the left. At the end of the alley, you'll see three soldiers off in the distance. Engage them with the Enfield. Around the corner and across the road to the west is a gazebo with a mounted machine gun. Like last time, throw a smoke grenade right in front of the gunner. Once his view is obstructed, move around to the left of the gazebo and gun him down with the Sten. Immediately move into the gazebo and get behind the machine gun. Enemy troops are moving toward your position from the south and the east. As soon as you can, open up on the soldiers before they get too close.

From the gazebo, move down the road heading east and turn your attention to the white building on the left. As you approach, a few soldiers inside open fire. Take cover on the opposite side of the road, and take them out one by one with the Enfield. When the action dies down, move into the building with the Sten drawn. Move into the

Use the machine gun in the gazebo to mow down the incoming troops.

room on the right and wait for a soldier to enter the room. Once he's down, move up the stairs he came from and gun down the soldier standing on the balcony. He'll fall through the railing, providing you an easy way to get down. But first, pull out your Enfield and engage the two soldiers across the way to the north. It's easier to take them out from up here than from the ground. You may have to side step to your left to see both of them.

The Train Station

When it's quiet and you're drawing no more fire, drop to the ground and move through the corridor ahead. A soldier rounds the corner to the left. Drop him before he can raise his weapon. Continue following this open passage around to the west until it leads to a metal workshop. Inside are two mechanics armed with pistols. Take them out, then quickly approach the eastern opening of the shop that faces the station platform. Pull out the Enfield and take position along the right side of the opening. From here, take out as many enemy soldiers as you can see.

More soldiers pour out of the northern offices. Keep an eye on them. Since the enemy holds a high position, you make a prime target for grenades. If a grenade is coming your direction, retreat farther into the workshop until it explodes, then move back to your previous position. Continue firing until you can no longer spot any enemies.

TIP

There's a first aid kit on a table inside the workshop.

When you can't see any more enemies, approach the ramp leading up to the station platform. The high concrete wall prevents you from seeing any of the troops waiting on the other side, so toss a grenade or two. Equip the Sten and move to the platform. If the grenades didn't get them, there may be two mechanics waiting for you. Drop them both with short bursts from the Sten.

Engage the enemy soldiers on the station platform from inside the metal workshop to the west. Watch out for incoming grenades.

77

Immediately turn to the north—facing the bridge. Two soldiers approach along the tracks. Gun them down. Pick up any dropped supplies around the station platform, then continue north along the right side of the tracks. Ahead and to the left, there's a soldier firing from behind a concrete wall. Take cover behind the destroyed artillery gun and use the Enfield to drop him with one shot. The approach to the bridge is now clear.

You have to plant four charges on the bridge—two on each side. The locations to place the charges are indicated by the usual red transparent charge symbol. With the Sten equipped, quickly move along the left side of the track until you spot the position for the first charge. Place it by pressing E and keep moving north to the next position.

Use the Sten to suppress the enemy while moving forward on the bridge to place the charges.

After placing the second charge, cross the tracks to place the third one. About this time, some enemy troops begin firing at you from farther down the bridge. Lay down some suppressing fire with the Sten and quickly place the third charge. Don't turn your back. Instead, backpedal along the right side of the tracks while firing the Sten at the approaching enemy troops—don't worry about accuracy.

Place the last charge and quickly move back to the Captain's position. As soon as the last charge is placed, the synchronized charge timers start counting down. Once you're next to the Captain, a cut scene shows the incoming train crossing the bridge just as the charges explode. Good work, solider!

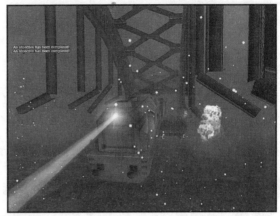

Once the charges are placed, move back to a safe distance, and watch the fireworks.

TIP

Don't take too long placing the charges. If you're too slow, the train will cross the bridge, resulting in a mission failure.

79

4

Assault in the Ardennes

The Hills of Bastogne

—Bernard J. McKearney, from the book *Rendezvous with Destiny: A History of the 101st Airborne Division* by Leonard Rapport and Arthur Northwood, Jr. Under license by Sean Konecky, Konecky & Konecky Books

The crops should be full in Belgium this year,

The soil should be fertile, but the price has been dear,

The wheat should be red on the hills of Bastogne

For its roots have been drenched by the blood of our own.

Battered and reeling we stand in their way,

It's here we are, and here we will stay.

Embittered, wrathful, we watch our pals fall,

God, where's the end, the end of it all?

Confident and powerful, they strike at our lines,

But we beat them back, fighting for time.

Berserk with fury, they are hitting us now,

Flesh against steel—we'll hold—but how?

For each day that we stay, more mothers must grieve.

For each hill that we hold more men must we leave.

Yes, honor the men who will some day come home,

But pray for the men 'neath the hills of Bastogne.

Into the Woods

December 24, 1944

Ardennes Forest

Belgium

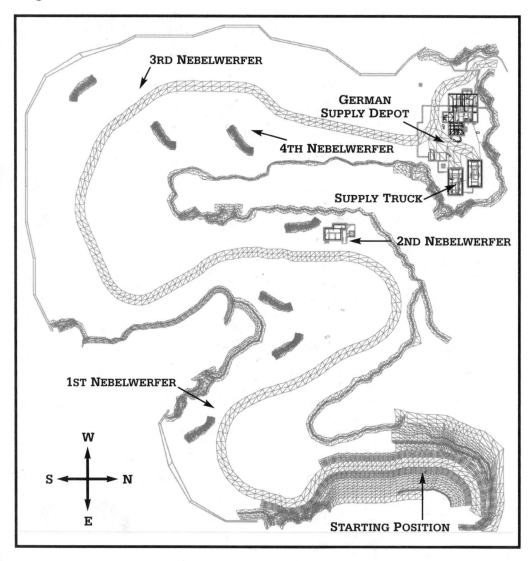

While attempting to capture a strategic town in the Ardennes, a group of U.S. soldiers has been cut off from Allied supply lines. You and your small squad have been ordered to steal a German supply truck and divert it to the isolated soldiers. Loaded with medical supplies, weapons, ammunition, and food, this truck represents the last hope for the men trapped in the snow-blanketed forest.

Your four-man squad must capture an enemy supply truck. Keep a watchful eye on your squadmates—they're not very good shots.

Camouflaged enemy infantry and tank patrols are a few of the obstacles you'll face when attempting this daring rescue operation.

INITIAL OBJECTIVE

• Acquire a supply truck

Follow the road south, then turn right facing a western clearing. You'll see three German soldiers moving toward you. They won't spot you immediately, so find a good position near the side of the road and get your M1 ready for action. As your squadmates file in behind you, they'll begin opening fire. Join in and drop the three soldiers before they know what hit them. Facing south,

Drop the three patrolling Germans before they take cover behind the trees.

approach their bodies to pick up some rifle ammo. Another soldier pops up over the hill ahead. Drop him with the Thompson.

83

> ## TIP
>
> There's a first aid kit behind some sandbags along the southeast road.

Move up the hill to the south, using trees for cover. Across the road is a Nebelwerfer attempting to hit your squad. There are also some entrenched Germans to the left. Find adequate cover and concentrate on taking out the soldiers in the trench. Once they're down, sidestep to the right to get a clear shot at the Nebelwerfer's operator. Drop him before the halftrack approaches from the northwest.

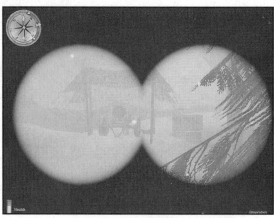

Don't reveal yourself to the Nebelwerfer. Take out its operator from a distance.

NEW OBJECTIVE

• Use Nebelwerfer to destroy the halftrack

> ## TIP
>
> Make sure your squadmates are behind you before operating the Nebelwerfer. It's a dangerous weapon, and you don't want to shoot them by mistake.

The halftrack is full of infantry, but your position on the hill gives you an advantage, allowing you to shoot down inside it. Keep this position until the halftrack is vacant. Once the area is clear, cross the road to the unoccupied Nebelwerfer. Move behind it and press E to operate it. As soon as you get behind its controls, three more soldiers appear on the hill where you were. The Nebelwerfer fires explosive rockets, so instead of trying to score direct hits, aim for their feet. Once the three soldiers are down, concentrate on taking out the halftrack. It should take four hits. Once the halftrack is destroyed, you get a new objective.

Use the Nebelwerfer on the enemy troops on the hill, then destroy the halftrack.

NEW OBJECTIVE

• Destroy four Nebelwerfers

One of your squadmates hands over some sticky bombs for use in the demolition of this and future Nebelwerfers. These work the same as explosive charges—find the flashing spot and press E to set the explosive. Plant the sticky bomb on the Nebelwerfer's wheel and get away before it detonates. Once it explodes, continue north, but stay off the road, moving along the slope on the left. Ahead you'll find another occupied trench overlooking the road below. Help your squad clear out the three enemy soldiers from a distance, then move in with the Thompson to seal the deal.

TIP

The Medic in your squad isn't armed, so make sure he's safe at all times. Although he isn't helpful during an assault, he dispenses medicinal canteens as your squad takes damage.

From the trench, go west over the hill to another trench with two soldiers. Take them out, then move forward to collect some ammo and a first aid kit. As you move into the trench, you hear another Nebelwerfer off in the distance and another soldier fires at you. Spot the soldier with your M1. Wait for your squad to catch up, then move west using the trees and rocks for cover.

85

Soldiers fire from the trench on the opposite side of the road. Use the large boulder straight ahead for cover. Now spot the wooden outpost to the north—this is the Nebelwerfer's location. With your left shoulder up against a boulder, aim at the large black tanks at the base of the tower. When you shoot them, they explode, taking out the Nebelwerfer and its operator.

Fire at the black flammable tanks near the Nebelwerfer to destroy it.

Next, take care of the sniper in the tower. He may be hard to see, so simply fire into the tower with the M1 and wait for the shooting to stop. Sidestep around the boulder and take out the two soldiers in the trench on the opposite side of the road. Cross the road and head for the trench—be ready to open fire on any survivors. Then, move over to the wooden outpost and climb the tower to retrieve the sniper's G43 and a first aid kit.

Return to the ground and proceed along the road heading south. Stay left and continue moving forward until you see an enemy tank moving in your direction.

Panzer Attack

> ### NEW OBJECTIVE
> - Use sticky bomb to destroy tank

Once you spot the tank ahead, immediately move to the right side of the road and crouch behind a rock next to the road. Use the Thompson to take down the two soldiers on either side of the road. As the

Don't fire at the tank's machine gunner until you're ready to apply a sticky bomb. Otherwise, the tank's main gun will begin to track you, making it difficult to move in close.

tank draws near, aim into the road and wait for it to appear. When the tank's turret comes into view, fire at the machine gunner with an aggressive burst, then immediately stand up and rush toward the tank. Attach a sticky bomb to the rear-left side of the tank and continue sidestepping to your right, moving behind the tank. As soon as you take out the machine gunner up top, the tank will track you with its main gun. Stay ahead of the turret's rotation to avoid getting blasted at close range. Continue strafing around the tank until the sticky bomb explodes.

TIP

Detonate sticky bombs early by shooting them. Just make sure you're standing back a good distance.

Continue moving along the right side of the road. Four soldiers positioned near some boulders fire at you. Use the M1 to take them out. Follow the path around, keeping the steep hill to your right and the road to your left. While rounding a corner, you come across two soldiers near a tree. Take them down. There's also a soldier on the hill above trying to drop grenades on you. Ignore him for now, but watch for his grenades.

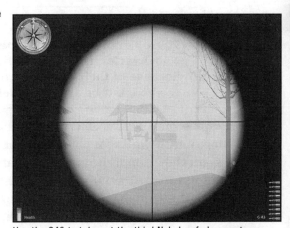
Use the G43 to take out the third Nebelwerfer's operator.

The third Nebelwerfer should now be in sight, but just out of range. Use your newly acquired G43 to spot the operator through the scope and fire.

Turn your attention to the soldier on the hill above. Either run up and gun him down, or lob a grenade in his direction. Either way, climb to where he was standing and grab some SMG ammo. From up here, you should see another trench to the northwest. Use the M1 to take out the soldiers inside. Move forward and clear out the trench, picking up supplies as you go.

87

Cross the road to take out the third Nebelwerfer. As you move toward the Nebelwerfer, four enemy soldiers approach from the east. Take them down before they inflict too much damage on you and your squad. Finally, place a charge on the Nebelwerfer and move away.

Slowly move up this hill and take out the final Nebelwerfer's operator from the side. Be careful not to expose yourself to the two soldiers in the trench below.

> **TIP**
> There's another trench southwest of the third Nebelwerfer. It's occupied by two soldiers. Because of their elevation, they may not even see you, but be aware of their presence.

Cross the road again, and move back to the trench. From there, head north until you hear the next Nebelwerfer hum into action. There's another trench between you and the final Nebelwerfer, but if you creep forward slowly, you see the operator without revealing yourself to the trench. Gun down the operator, then inch forward to take out the two soldiers in the trench. As you move into the trench, you'll notice another German tank on the road to the left.

Approaching the Compound

NEW OBJECTIVE

• Use sticky bomb to destroy second tank

Immediately move behind the controls of the Nebelwerfer and aim just beyond the tank in front of you. The tank can't elevate its main gun to engage you, so focus your first attack on the various soldiers firing at you from the opposite side of the road. Aim for their feet and watch as they fly into the air. Once they're down, aim at the tank. It'll take five direct hits before the tank begins to smolder.

The soldiers on the other side of the road pose a bigger threat than the tank. Take them out, then pound away on the tank.

Stay behind the Nebelwerfer and wait for the tank crew to climb out. Take them out before they have a chance to run off into the woods. With the tank and surrounding opposition neutralized, plant a sticky bomb on the last Nebelwerfer and move away.

Make sure none of these soldiers gets behind the machine gun nest in front of the gate.

Take out four more enemy soldiers while moving north along the road leading into the supply compound. As you get close, an enemy truck crosses in front of the front gate and spins out of control. As this happens, take a position along the rock face on the right side of the road. Four soldiers eventually climb out and begin firing in your direction.

There's a unoccupied machine gun nest to the left of the gate—make sure it stays that way. Use the G43 to view the actions of the soldiers and take out any that move toward the machine gun nest; at least one tries. Once the four soldiers are down, approach the front gates.

> **TIP**
>
> If you move behind the machine gun nest, several troops materialize from the south. Gun them down or, if you don't want to deal with them, simply move around the front of the sandbags.

The Supply Depot

At the front gates, move along the fence to your right and follow it until you come to an opening leading into the compound. Peek around the corner to spot your first enemy and open fire. Stay behind the corner and wait for the soldiers to come to you. Gun them down with the Thompson as they round the corner.

Peek around this corner, and engage the enemies guarding the supply depot. Your squad at the front gate helps draw their attention away from you.

When the courtyard looks clear, move toward the sandbags between the two wooden sheds. A soldier appears in the upper window of the house. Gun him down before he has a chance to throw a grenade at you.

> **TIP**
>
> You also can enter the supply depot by moving through the house. However, there's no real advantage in taking this route. Sneaking around the fence to the back allows you to draw all the enemy soldiers into one concentrated area, which makes them easier to gun down, especially if your squadmates help engage them from the front gate.

Turn around and look at the two wooden sheds. The one on the left holds a tank and two soldiers guarding it from a catwalk above. It's not necessary to enter this shed at all unless you want to use one of your sticky bombs on the tank. If you do decide to take out this tank, quickly move in, attach a sticky bomb, and move out. The explosion takes out the two soldiers above.

The shed on the right contains the supply truck you've come to steal. Before opening the door, equip yourself with a hand grenade. As you open the door, toss the grenade into the back right corner of the shed. This should take out at least two of the soldiers guarding the truck. Switch to the Thompson and open fire on the other soldiers inside. There are two on the catwalk above and four on the ground. When the shed is clear, move in behind the truck to complete your objective.

Be ready to throw a grenade into the back right corner of this shed to take out a few soldiers. That's the supply truck you've been looking for on the left.

The Greatest Escape

NEW OBJECTIVE

• Escort the supply truck to the allied line

It wasn't easy to survive the threats in the forest, but your team finally tracked down the precious supply truck. Now things really get tricky. While another team member commandeers the truck, you jump into the back of an enemy halftrack and provide escort.

Blasting away with the halftrack's anti-tank gun, you run a gauntlet of Nazi firepower before delivering the supplies to the cut-off U.S. soldiers. It's up to you to protect the truck at all costs.

The halftrack's PzB41 anti-tank gun has unlimited ammo, so don't hold back.

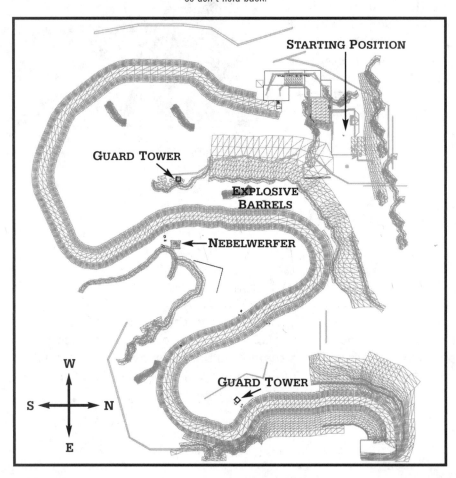

STARTING POSITION

GUARD TOWER

EXPLOSIVE BARRELS

NEBELWERFER

GUARD TOWER

W
S — N
E

Target Priorities

1. Tanks

2. Halftracks

3. Panzerschreck soldiers

4. Guard towers

5. Infantry

The first tank appears beyond the trees to your left. Aim for the turret to take it down quickly.

As you leave the supply depot, the halftrack hits the soldier running out of the guard post, so don't bother firing. As you move east, fire on the three soldiers straight ahead— one on the road and two others on the hill above.

When the halftrack turns south, concentrate on the left side of the road. Fire at two soldiers running by until you spot the first tank in the distance. As soon as you see it, open fire on the turret, where the armor is thinnest. Once that tank is burning, turn right to engage another one moving behind the trees. The halftrack makes another turn along a trench occupied by a couple of soldiers, including one with a Panzerschreck. Take them out.

> ## TIP
> This mission is extremely difficult, but succeeding is a matter of knowing where and when to shoot. There's only one automatic save spot, so consider saving the game yourself, especially after difficult sections.

Top of the Mountain

The halftrack comes to a halt at the edge of a steep downward slope. While it's teetering over the ledge, fire on the enemies below. Off to the left is a Nebelwerfer and a couple of soldiers. To the right, just behind the large pine tree, is a Panzerschreck soldier. Take out these threats from up here before the halftrack slides down the mountain.

93

At the bottom of the hill, take out this guard tower.

At the bottom, immediately turn toward the guard tower just behind you and take it out. Otherwise, its machine gun will eat away at you as you pass it later. While the halftrack backs up, keep the gun facing aft and wait for a tank to come into view in the distance. As soon as you see it, open fire. The tank momentarily disappears behind a ridge and then reappears directly behind you. Keep firing until it explodes.

Don't let this tank sneak up behind you.

TIP

Don't ignore soldiers. Although you're in an armored vehicle, they'll still find a way to hit you, especially if they're firing from an elevated position.

94

Swivel the gun around to face forward. Eliminate the troops harassing the supply truck by firing a few rounds near the boulder to the left of the road. About this time, a German JU-87 swoops down and drops a bomb. It doesn't do any damage, but it does down a tree blocking the road ahead. The halftrack moves left along the snow bank, taking a detour around the fallen tree. This lines you up with a long trench occupied by a couple of soldiers. Take them out before they open fire on you. At the far end of the trench are a few explosive barrels. Aim at them and wait for a German tank to pass by. When the timing is right, fire at the barrels, causing them to explode. Immediately train your sights on the tank to destroy it.

Shooting the explosive barrels damages the tank, but probably won't take it out. Follow through with a few point-blank shots.

TIP

Shoot the explosive barrels from a distance. If you wait too long, the explosions can damage your halftrack as well as the enemy tank.

Aim the gun forward up the next hill. Along the left side are two soldiers and a halftrack. Concentrate on destroying the halftrack, then mop up the soldiers. Next, dip down across the main road and climb another hill. At the top are two soldiers. The one on the left has a Panzerschreck, and the other is equipped with a submachine gun. Take them out before you get too close.

95

At the top of the hill be prepared to take on another German tank at close range. You'll have to track the tank while your halftrack turns in a new direction. When it comes into view, keep firing at its turret until it explodes. Immediately aim forward and open fire on another tank heading in your direction. Once it explodes, take out the soldiers next to it.

Avoid toe-to-toe confrontations with tanks. You're at an obvious disadvantage.

The Home Stretch

The halftrack eventually returns to the main road. Fire at the soldiers in the trench ahead before they get too close to be dangerous. Next, turn the gun aft to spot another halftrack moving in behind the supply truck. Hit its side armor before it gets directly behind the supply truck, obscuring your view. Once it's down, take out the guard tower on the left side of the road. Just beyond it is another halftrack—take it out quickly.

Take out this halftrack before it moves in behind the supply truck.

Turn the gun aft and spot the soldier with the Panzerschreck on the ledge above. After taking him out, swing the gun forward to look for one more enemy tank along the left side of the road. Destroy it and swing the gun to the back in search of more targets.

You should begin seeing Allied soldiers along the road, aiding your escape. The path is finally clear.

After taking out the guard tower, look for another halftrack on the other side of the hill.

A Night in Hell

After escorting the supply truck to your fellow soldiers, you're all finally sitting around enjoying some of the hard-won spoils of combat. In a flash, the scene turns to chaos. A barrage of enemy shells shatters the nighttime quiet, and you're in the midst of an all-out firefight.

Keep an eye on the foxhole below. That's where to be when the shelling starts.

With German infantry and tanks storming across the open field, you need to think fast. Use whatever it takes to stop the advance—pick off enemy soldiers one at a time with your rifle, mow them down with a submachine gun, and take out the Tiger Tanks with a bazooka.

97

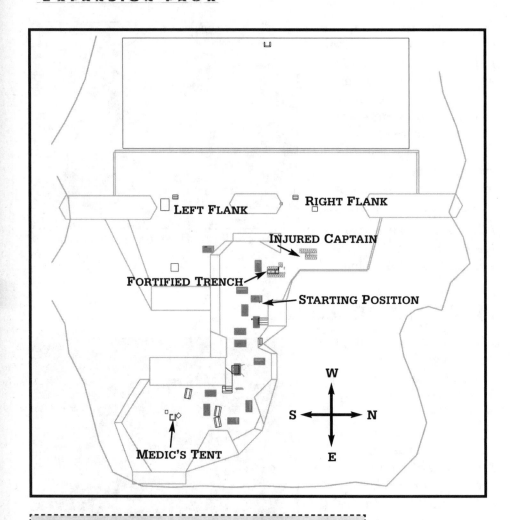

LEFT FLANK

RIGHT FLANK

INJURED CAPTAIN

FORTIFIED TRENCH

STARTING POSITION

W

S — N

E

MEDIC'S TENT

NEW OBJECTIVE

• Get orders from the Captain at the front line

TIP

As long as you're in a foxhole, there's no reason to crouch. Instead, remain standing and ready to run.

As soon as the artillery barrage begins, jump in the nearest foxhole with the other two soldiers. Wait until the shelling dies down and you receive the objective to get to the Captain. This places a heading indicator on your compass, pointing northwest. Follow the heading to a trench reinforced with wood planks. Crawl through it to find the injured Captain on the other side. As long as you don't deviate from this path, you get to the Captain without any more incoming barrages.

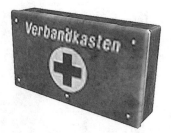

TIP

The opening sequences of this mission are timed, so move to your objectives quickly. Once you receive your first objective, you only have about 30 seconds to get to the Captain. From the Captain's position, you have just under three minutes to find the Medic. Once you find the Medic, you have about another three minutes to get back to the Captain.

You have a limited time to find the injured Captain. If you don't get to him fast enough, he'll die.

Medic!

NEW OBJECTIVE

• Locate the Medic

The Captain is wounded and will die if he doesn't receive immediate medical attention. Don't stand around waiting for your objective to change—immediately turn back to the fortified trench and wait there for the next barrage to die down. As your objective changes, the

compass heading changes to
southeast. From here, spot
the covered foxhole just ahead
and run to it as soon as the
barrage halts momentarily.
Pick up the rifle rounds next
to this trench and face east.

Ahead is a series of
foxholes you'll need to use for
taking cover. At the end of the
current barrage, move forward
to the next covered foxhole on
the left. It's hard to see the

From the fortified trench near the Captain, head for the
covered foxhole to the southeast.

next foxhole from this position, but at the end of the next barrage,
continue moving east until you spot an uncovered trench to your
right. Another soldier is running for it, too, but he won't make it.
Inside and around this foxhole you'll find a medicinal canteen and
some machine gun ammo that are valuable later.

Look for the next covered foxhole (with the green tarp) dead
ahead. Move to it during the next lull. Inside is a first aid kit. While
still facing east, inch forward until you can see an uncovered foxhole
below—this is where you want to go next. As you move forward,
another solider gets taken out right in front of the foxhole you're
heading for.

Turn south to face a row
of logs and a truck in the
distance. Move to the next
covered foxhole (next to the
logs) and wait for another halt
in the shelling. When it's clear,
move around the left of the
logs and into the occupied
foxhole on the other side.
Straight ahead you should see
the Medic's tent. Move toward
him as soon as it's clear. He'll
drop what he's doing and
follow you back to the Captain.

Get to the Medic as soon as possible. He'll follow you
back to the Captain's position.

Save the Captain

NEW OBJECTIVE

• Escort Medic to the Captain

The Medic can't save this poor chap, but he leaves behind an StG 44. Now aren't you glad you picked up that machine gun ammo?

As you turn to head back to the Captain, an enemy plane swoops down for a strafing run, injuring a solider near a foxhole to the north. Move over to the injured solider. The Medic will try to save him, but he's already gone. While the Medic is working on him, grab the soldier's StG 44 and the nearby medicinal canteen. Once you have the items, hop into the foxhole and wait for another break in the barrage. Head north to the uncovered foxhole, and turn to face west. From here move to the covered foxhole on the hill on the left. If you didn't get it before, use the first aid kit inside. Next, move to the uncovered foxhole to the right and wait.

Still facing west, move to the covered foxhole along the right. At the next opportunity, quickly run to the last covered foxhole along the left. From here, you can see the fortified trench to the north—you're almost there! Wait out the next barrage and make a break for the trench.

Wait in the trench for the next barrage to pass, then quickly move to the Captain. The Medic goes to work on the Captain as the artillery strike dies down. Suddenly, gunfire erupts through the woods to the west. The enemy is attacking your lines!

The Medic tends to the Captain's wounds. But don't get comfortable—the enemy attack is just beginning.

101

Holding the Line

Immediately move northwest until you find a shallow trench in the snow—this is the right flank. German troops are approaching from the west in an attempt to overrun your line. Hold this position and eliminate the attackers.

Help your buddies turn back the German forces on the right flank.

The StG 44 machine gun comes in handy here. Although it's fully automatic, fire in two- to three-round bursts while aiming at the upper torsos of your enemies—this is usually more than enough to take them out. Whatever you do, keep the enemy from advancing past the trench. As soon as an enemy soldier touches the eastern side, the mission is over. Continue firing at the attackers until they begin to retreat.

TIP
There's a first aid kit in the right flank trench and some Panzerschreck rounds nearby.

TIP

For the most part, the German attackers won't fire on you until they're at close range. However, you'll need to watch out for friendly fire if one of the attackers makes his way into the trench. Your buddies will frantically fire at the intruder without taking your presence into account. The best strategy is to keep the enemy in front of you at all times.

Once the Germans retreat from the right flank, turn south to find the left flank. The right flank trench ends near some woods, so move around to the left, through the trees, until you find the left flank trench. Here, you'll find some more friendly soldiers in need of assistance. Run in behind the trench, collecting the Panzerschreck and ammo as you move.

Move to the left flank and defend it from another wave of attackers.

Take a position toward the middle of the trench, where the incoming assault is heaviest. Immediately open up with the StG 44 until the first wave of enemy troops falls. Quickly move to the far left of the trench and pick up a box of machine gun ammo and a couple of Panzerschreck rounds. Return to the center of the trench and continue firing at the advancing enemies. Before long, you'll hear the rumbling of an approaching tank. Keep firing at the incoming troops until it comes into view. Pull up the Panzerschreck and fire at the tank—it takes a couple of shots to destroy it. Once the tank is down, switch back to one of your guns and return to the right flank.

TIP

If you don't destroy the tank quickly, it'll cross the line, immediately ending the mission.

103

NEW OBJECTIVE

• Return and defend the right flank

> **TIP**
>
> You may notice a Granatwerfer positioned behind the right flank's trench. You can try to use it against the advancing attackers, but your guns are more effective for this engagement.

When you get back to the right flank, a tank approaches the far left of the trench. Don't worry about it—another soldier with a Panzerschreck takes it out. Move to an open spot in the center of the trench and get ready for the next assault. While you're waiting, equip your Panzerschreck and make sure a new round is loaded. Now switch back to the StG 44 and mow down the approaching troops. This wave includes a few soldiers with Panzerschrecks of their own. Take them out before they fire into your line.

When another enemy tank draws near, use the Panzerschreck to destroy it. Aim for the turret to destroy it with one hit. If you've got the time, load another round into the Panzerschreck before switching back to one of your other guns.

Continue engaging the infantry until a halftrack approaches along the far right side of your position. Immediately pull up the Panzerschreck to destroy it. As soon as the halftrack is defeated, the enemy troops retreat.

Good job—you've successfully held off the enemy attack.

Use the Panzerschreck to destroy the enemy tank and halftrack advancing on the right flank.

> **TIP**
>
> If you run out of ammo for the StG 44, switch to the MP-40. It does less damage, but its automatic fire is good for close-range combat.

What Comes Around...

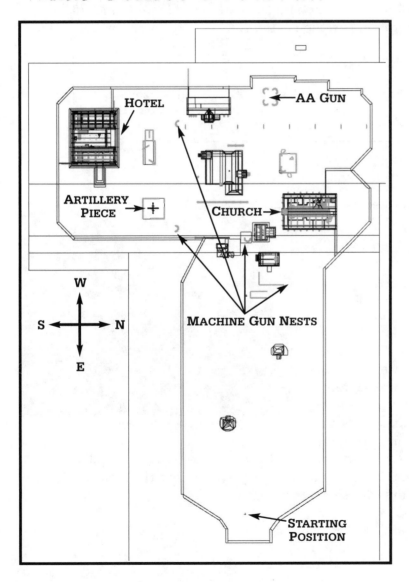

Having survived the enemy assault, you and the other troops advance on a town being used as a base of operations for an artillery company. Just a few hours earlier, the enemy attempted to cross a field and penetrate your lines. Now, you must cross that same field and enter the occupied town.

It's your job to go building-by-building and room-by-room to rid the town of Nazis. Just when you think you have things under control, you'll have to deal with the early morning strafing runs of a Luftwaffe fighter. Not the best way to spend Christmas morning.

> ### TIP
> You begin this mission with the same weapons and ammunition that you had at the end of the previous mission.

Crossing the Field

INITIAL OBJECTIVE

• Cross the field alive

Although the Captain tells you to follow him up the middle of the field, doing so will get you killed. To start off, follow the Captain out of the first crater and move toward the embankment to the left as he throws a smoke grenade. While up against this embankment,

Listen to your Captain's instruction, then take action.

you'll be safe from artillery fire. Find a space between artillery explosions and run forward and to the right, into the same crater where the Captain's smoke grenade landed.

TIP

Don't let the quick pace of the battle throw off your judgment. Take the time to maneuver from crater to crater. Rushing across the field will only result in a quick death.

The tank is usually destroyed by the time you reach this point. If it isn't, take it out with your Panzerschreck.

Note the tank off in the distance to the right. It doesn't pose a threat to you from here, but you need to approach it. Leapfrog into the next couple of craters until you're in one just to the left of the tank. The tank may have been destroyed by now, but if not, take it out with the Panzerschreck.

Next, move to the tan rock straight ahead and pick up a first aid kit and some Panzerschreck rounds.

Into the Town!

NEW OBJECTIVE

• Find the Captain

This machine gunner must be taken out before you can move into the town.

Once you're behind the rock, you're safe from the artillery fire. Concentrate on taking out the troops defending the town ahead. Pull out your Mauser and sidestep around the left side of the rock. Keep moving into the clear until you spot a machine gun nest to the right.

The gunner is usually too busy shooting at your buddies to notice you. Quickly take aim and drop him with a shot to the head. When he's down, pick off other enemy soldiers from this position before moving forward.

107

Move toward the house straight ahead. There's an enemy soldier inside shooting through the windows. If you can't spot him from a distance, move in close and equip an automatic weapon of your choice. Move toward the house and peek through the windows. If you still can't see him, throw open the door and gun him down. Inside on a table is a first aid kit, a Panzerschreck, and some Panzerschreck ammo.

Head through the back door to find the Captain inside a partially destroyed barn. If he hasn't already, help him take out the machine gun nest to the northwest. Once the gunner is down, follow the Captain to the church.

The Church

NEW OBJECTIVE

• Clear church

As the Captain enters the church, follow him. Make sure you have an automatic weapon ready. If you have ammo, the StG 44 is a good choice.

Help the Captain take out this machine gun nest covering the entrance to the church.

Some crates inside are obscuring your view of the bottom floor. Sidestep to the right until you make contact with the enemy. There are three soldiers on the bottom floor. Help the Captain defeat them, then follow him up the stairs at the back of the room, ready to open fire. Two enemy soldiers are waiting for you at the top of the stairs. Take them down quickly.

Two more soldiers are at the far end of the room. One is shooting out a window onto the street below. Eliminate them both.

> ### TIP
>
> The Captain is more of a liability than an asset. If he dies, the mission is over. Keep an eye out for him.

Climb the crates to reach the broken ladder leading to the church steeple. Climb the ladder and slowly approach the far end to find the sniper who's firing at your buddies. Gun him down and take his rifle, a KAR98 Sniper.

With the new rifle in hand, peek out each of the three windows and pick off a few soldiers below. You can usually find a couple of soldiers with Panzerschrecks firing at the church. When you can't find any more targets, head down the ladder. There are a couple of first aid kits on either side of the crates.

Use your new sniper rifle to take out the enemies below.

Follow the Captain through the front door of the church. You now have a new objective.

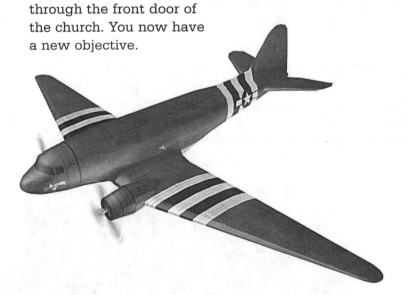

The Hotel

NEW OBJECTIVE

• Clear hotel

With the sniper rifle still in hand, follow the Captain along the road leading to the hotel. Just ahead on the left is a machine gun nest. Quickly look through the scope of the rifle and take out the machine gunner before he opens fire.

Switch to an automatic weapon and move toward the artillery position straight ahead. There's a tank circling around to the right, but ignore that for now. Gun down the two soldiers nearby, and move into the destroyed structure to man the gun. Quickly swing the barrel around and point it at the tank—it should be heading toward you now. Fire one shell to take it out.

Use the 88mm gun to take out the tank patrolling in front of the hotel.

TIP

Try using grenades to clear some of the smaller rooms.

Follow the Captain to the hotel entrance, dispatching a couple enemy soldiers along the way. In the doorway is a shotgun. Grab it, but switch back to an automatic weapon before entering. The Captain stays out front while you enter to clear the hotel. Take out the two soldiers in the first room with short bursts, then move through the door on the right. After entering, immediately turn right and take out the soldier standing in the far corner.

Cautiously move up the stairs and take out the solider at the top. Equip the shotgun and conduct a room-to-room search along the hallway to the left. There's a soldier in the middle room, a medicinal canteen in the room next door, and two soldiers in the large room at the end of the hall. Switch to an automatic weapon, retrace your steps to the stairs, and take the door to the left. There's a lone soldier shooting out the window to the left. Sneak up behind him and take him out.

The shotgun is great for clearing the small rooms in the hotel.

117

In the same room, begin moving up the stairs. Hold halfway up the steps until you can see a couple of soldiers. Once you take them out, head upstairs and take out the soldier standing in the corner waiting to ambush you. Move to that corner and pick up two first aid kits, a box of machine gun ammo, and a box of grenades.

This impressive cache of supplies is located on the third floor of the hotel.

Move down to the previous room and through the door ahead. Be ready to gun down a couple of soldiers. Equip the shotgun for another room-to-room search along the hallway. You should find three soldiers. Next, move downstairs leading to the ground floor. Take out the two soldiers in this room to complete your objective.

TIP

There are 18 enemy soldiers inside the hotel. Your objective is achieved when all of them are neutralized.

Securing the Town

NEW OBJECTIVE

• Find the Captain

Leave the hotel through the door where you entered. The Captain isn't around, so you'll have to go find him again. But before you take any steps forward, sidestep to the left and peer through the KAR98's scope to spot a machine gun nest in the distance. Take out the gunner before moving any farther.

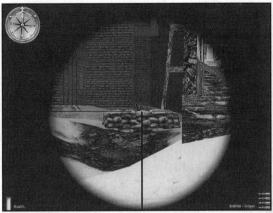

Take out the machine gunner as soon as you exit the hotel. If you move any closer, he'll open fire.

Move toward the now-unoccupied machine gun nest and continue along the road heading north. Along the way, take out the single soldier who ambushes you from the left.

Keep moving north. Eventually, you'll see an enemy halftrack straight ahead. Don't bother shooting at it—your buddies will take it out. Among the large group of friendly soldiers ahead is the Captain. As you meet up with the Captain, a German Stuka JU-87 streaks across the sky.

113

NEW OBJECTIVE

- Destroy Stuka with artillery

Immediately move to the AA gun emplacement to the west, and train your sights on the sky. The Stuka flies in a predictable flight path from left to right, and along the same path from right to left. As long as you keep your aim along this path, you should have no problem hitting the enemy plane. Remember, the AA gun takes a while to warm up, so open fire before the plane comes into view. If you wait until you see the plane, it'll streak past you before the guns can fire up.

The Stuka is fast, so warm up the guns before it flies in front of you.

With each pass, the Stuka strafes and drops a bomb, causing damage to your men below. If you fail to take the plane down quickly, the Captain will get killed, ending your mission. As you hit the plane, it begins trailing smoke. Keep firing at it during subsequent passes until it crashes. Finally, you and your battle-weary men control the town. Good job!

5
The Fall of Berlin

That Something

—by Ronald Tee, 56th Recce Regiment, Battleaxe Division, British 8th Army, from the book *A British Soldier Remembers*; ron@britishsoldier.com

It's funny, how one can lie,

and remember things of days gone by.

And in perhaps one short minute,

recapture a past year and all that's in it.

It's funny, how a quiet room, gives chance to ponder,

leading our thoughts, or even a funny phrase,

will recall something that happened in bye gone days.

Everyone stores up things that have past,

some are forgotten, others will always last.

But a soldier who has been to war,

has in life's memory book, something more.

"Something" that can only be,

in the memories of men, like you and me.

"Something" that is born midst shot and shell,

develops and grows in times of bloody hell.

This "comradeship" as it is known by us,

of which we never make much fuss.

Is this "something" which in our minds was set

in lands where many are lying yet.

And so I remember from the start,

the lads I knew, now far apart

my soldiering is finished, I leave it all behind,

but that "something" comes with me in my mind.

A Traitor Among Us

Berlin

Heart of the German Empire

0430 Hours

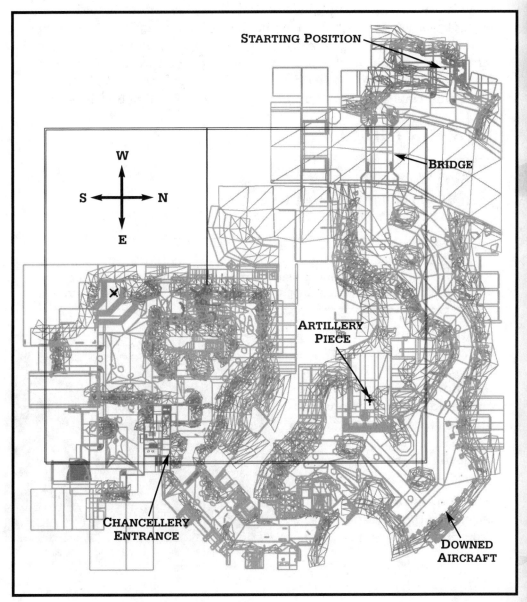

STARTING POSITION

BRIDGE

W
S — N
E

ARTILLERY PIECE

CHANCELLERY ENTRANCE

DOWNED AIRCRAFT

117

The German forces have been routed on all fronts. All that remains is Berlin, the still-pumping heart of the once-mighty German war machine. American and British forces have ceased their advance, conceding the capture of the city to the Russian Red Army.

Before the final assault, you're ordered into the city to uncover vital documents, including lists of double agents, traitors, and corrupt politicians. The Russians have grudgingly agreed to give you a small window of time to retrieve what you can before they launch a full-scale assault on the city. Don't be long, though. The Red Army isn't as interested in these documents as it is in crushing the last remaining Nazi stronghold and bringing the Third Reich to its knees.

Into the City!

INITIAL OBJECTIVE

• Cross the bridge and enter Berlin

TIP

You begin this mission armed exclusively with Soviet weapons, including the famed PPSh41 submachine gun.

The mission begins as you stand around a group of Russian soldiers talking about the impending assault on the city. Suddenly, explosions and gunfire erupt around you. One of the Soviet soldiers tells you to move into the city immediately.

Before setting off on your own, help the Soviet troops fight off the attackers. Next,

Help your comrades fight off the attackers in the east before entering the city.

move toward the street to the east, and turn south. You'll see two bridges in the distance— cross the closest one. Pull up the SVT 40 sniper rifle and peer through the scope. Three soldiers are positioned behind some concrete barriers on this side of the bridge, and another is positioned on the bridge in the distance—take all four of them out before going any farther. Your Soviet comrades help engage them. A couple of them drop medicinal canteens.

Move south to one of the concrete blocks on the western side of the bridge. Wait here for an enemy soldier to come into view on the other side. If you don't see him, move forward and look to the left, along the bank of the river. Drop him before he can open fire with his submachine gun. Once he's down, slowly move forward along the right side of the bridge. Next to the truck ahead is another soldier with his back turned—

Eliminate the machine gunner to the east while you're still on the bridge. He'll have a hard time hitting you at this range.

shoot him before moving closer. This will trigger a machine gunner at the far end of the street to open fire. Quickly pull up the SVT 40 and drop him before he hits you—though you should be pretty safe at this range, especially if you keep the truck in front of you.

Move along the right of the bridge to the truck ahead. If you need it, the soldier standing next to the truck dropped a medicinal canteen. You're now in the city—be careful and watch out for snipers.

Welcome to Berlin

NEW OBJECTIVE

• Locate downed aircraft and map to Chancellery

TIP

The rain extinguishes the lit fuses on the sticky bomb. You'll have to back off and shoot the bomb to make it detonate. The white plume of smoke emanating from the smoldering fuse makes it easy to spot from a distance.

Although it's not necessary, you can now destroy the truck with a sticky bomb. However, you'll have to shoot the bomb once it's attached because the rain extinguishes the fuse. Just make sure you stand back a good distance before shooting it. Once the truck is destroyed, quickly move to the machine gun nest you neutralized earlier—another truck is approaching. Get behind the sandbags and watch the truck move toward the bridge, where it stops. A couple of soldiers get out of the back and stand guard. If you open fire, the driver also gets out. Taking out these soldiers and their truck is purely optional. Then again, you don't get many opportunities to take open shots like this with a mounted machine gun. Grab the satchel of sticky bombs in the machine gun nest and continue moving north.

Before moving too far, turn east until you see the red glow of a burning barrel on one of the exposed upper story floors. On this floor, a soldier is positioned behind some sandbags. Peer through the SVT 40's scope to get a better view. As long as you don't get too close, he won't fire on you—make your shot count.

The burning barrel makes this enemy easy to spot.

Follow the road heading southeast until you can see a large open courtyard area. In the distance, you should be able to spot a lone sniper standing on the roof of a tall gray building. Take a shot and watch him fall off the building. The sound of your rifle alerts a three-man mortar crew just to your right. They won't fire the mortar at you, but they will try to hit you with small arms fire. Drop them quickly.

You now hear a German tank moving up the road behind you. There are two soldiers with rifles riding on each side. Equip your PPSh41 and make sure it has enough ammo. Move to the left side of the road and wait for the tank to get close. Instead of waiting for it to stop, move to the left rear position and attach a sticky bomb. Now use your PPSh41 to shoot the soldier on the left while

You'll have to attach then shoot the sticky bomb to destroy this tank.

backpedaling away from the tank. When you're back far enough, fire at the bomb to destroy the tank. If the soldier on the other side jumped off before the tank exploded, you'll have to gun him down, too. Approach the right side of the destroyed tank and pull up the SVT 40 while facing east. Look for the red glow of another burning barrel ahead—there's another sniper to take out.

> **TIP**
>
> As soon as the tank stops, its main gun will begin tracking you. If you need to, circle-strafe around the tank, staying ahead of the turret's rotation. Continue moving away from the tank and fire at the sticky bomb as soon as it comes into view.

121

Once the sniper is down, move toward the now-unoccupied Granatwerfer position to the right of the road. Another truck with two soldiers will approach and stop right in front of you. Use the PPSh41 to gun them down—don't forget the driver, too. If you want, attach a sticky bomb to the truck, following the usual routine to destroy it. Move back to the Granatwerfer and press E to operate it.

Use the Granatwerfer to clear the area next to the downed American aircraft.

Locate the truck in the distance parked next to the downed American aircraft—this is where you need to go. There are two soldiers standing on the other side of the truck; use the mortar to take them out. Begin by lowering the mortar all the way down, reducing its range and trajectory. Now point it in the direction of the truck. Once things are lined up, fire a round. The first round will probably take out the two soldiers, but keep firing rounds until the truck explodes.

From the Granatwerfer's position, move north across the road and up against the rubble. With the PPSh41 ready to fire, side step right. You'll find another sniper crouched on the rubble above—don't give him a chance to respond.

Go to the southeast pile of rubble, then turn your attention to the truck across the southwest open area. Two soldiers come running from this direction. Use the SVT 40 to take them out from a distance.

Circle around the same rubble pile until you can see a lone sniper off in the distance to the southwest. He'll probably see you before you see him. If you have trouble spotting him, find the truck and look above it. He's standing on a pile of rubble. When you take him out, move to the downed plane and retrieve the map. Press E to pick it up.

Clear the area of snipers and other soldiers before retrieving the map from the crash site.

TIP

Spotting enemy snipers in the dark city can be tough. While taking cover, look for muzzle flashes. These flashes not only illuminate the end of the sniper's rifle, but also the surrounding area. Once you determine the general direction of the sniper, aim toward the muzzle flashes, then switch to your scope view to fine tune your aim.

Finding the Chancellery

NEW OBJECTIVE

• Locate the Chancellery building

With the map in hand (and a new compass heading), move to the large classical structure with pillars to the southwest. As you approach, you'll hear the squeaking wheels of a nearby tank.

123

Fortunately, there's a flak cannon just inside the building. Before taking out the tank with the flak cannon, clear the nearby office where two soldiers are waiting. While running forward, toss a grenade in the open doorway, then equip the PPSh41. When the grenade explodes, move in and finish the job.

Use the flak cannon to destroy the tank and the truck.

Move back to the flak cannon and get behind its controls. By now the tank has stopped with its main gun pointed in your direction. Take aim at the turret and fire. It may take a couple of shots to destroy it. While you're there, destroy the truck to the right for more fireworks.

Use the machine gun to mow down the incoming troops. You won't be able to see them all from this position.

Move through the office area to your right (picking up some more sticky bombs along the way) and work your way around the corridor until you exit on the other side behind a machine gun nest. Move in behind the gun and take aim at a small squad of German troops approaching from the southeast. When they're down, exit the machine gun nest by side stepping left—there may be some stragglers you couldn't see from the machine gun's position. Finish them off with the SVT 40.

124

Switch back to the PPSh41 and move toward the building straight ahead. A soldier will pop out of a window above—don't let him surprise you.

Some of the crew may have survived. Be ready to gun them down.

As you round the corner to the east, another tank comes rolling over the pile of rubble dead ahead. Move back around the corner and wait for it to pass in front of you. Run up and slap a sticky bomb on its side and backpedal so you're behind the tank. When you're far enough back, open fire with the PPSh41 to detonate the sticky bomb. Don't turn your back on the tank just yet—a few survivors may climb out of the hatch. Be ready to gun them down.

Once the tank and its crew are taken care of, move through the rubble-filled alley to the east. Stop short of the road and take out a couple of enemy soldiers—one on a balcony ahead and another standing across the street to the right.

TIP

A safer alternative for taking out the tank is to let it pass you completely, then backtrack to the flak cannon to take it out. The tank should stop right next to the tank you previously destroyed. Either way, keep an eye out for surviving crew members.

Straight ahead is a car parked in front of a building with a brown door. It may look inconspicuous, but there are some good supplies on the other side of that door, as well as two enemy soldiers and an officer. Cross the street while equipping a grenade. Approach the door without moving next to any of the windows. When you're in position, open the door from the left side (without revealing yourself) and toss in the grenade. The room is fairly small, so expect the

125

grenade to do some
damage to the occupants
inside. After it explodes,
rush in and gun down any
of the still dazed survivors
with the PPSh41.

Inside you'll find a field
surgeon pack, a medicinal
canteen, another stash of
sticky bombs, and some
ammo the soldiers dropped.
Your aggressive actions
haven't gone unnoticed. A
soldier in the street outside

Toss the grenade into the center of the room for optimal effect.
Be ready to gun down any survivors.

may attempt to shoot at you through one of the windows. If you can
see him, fire a quick burst of automatic fire from inside. Otherwise,
step out of the door and shoot him.

Step outside and look southwest. There's another sniper at the far
end of the street, on the balcony of an orange building. Line up your
shot with the SVT 40 and fire. Once he's down, move down the
street and take cover behind some concrete blocks while a truck
approaches. It stops just ahead of your position.

Wait until the driver and
two soldiers get out, then
walk around the left of the
truck and place a sticky
bomb on the passenger
side door. Carefully walk
back to your previous
hiding spot and detonate
the explosive with the
PPSh41. The truck will
explode, eliminating the
driver and one of the
soldiers—take out the
other soldier as he
moves forward.

Destroy the truck while the enemies are standing next to it.

126

> ### TIP
>
> You can walk by holding down left ⌈Shift⌉ while moving. Walking produces less sound than running—ideal for sneaking around.

Once the truck is destroyed, turn your attention to the exposed orange building to the northwest. There's a sniper on the second floor waiting for you to move into his sights. While facing the building, slowly back up until you can see the top of his head, then fire. The area opposite the archway ahead is full of threats, including a tank and multiple snipers. Bypass these threats entirely by running through the arch and immediately turning left, heading for the wooden door—this leads into the Chancellery.

> ### TIP
>
> If you choose to stay and fight at the archway, you'll have to contend with a tank, three soldiers, and at least two well-concealed snipers at the opposite end of the street. It's not extremely challenging to take on these threats, it's just not necessary.

Retrieve the Documents

> **NEW OBJECTIVE**
>
> • Locate the safe containing list of double agents

Once you're inside the building, you won't have to worry about the enemies outside. Move to the staircase and pause at the base of the steps. A soldier will come into view above; gun him down with the PPSh41. Cautiously move up the stairs and get ready to engage

The PPSh41 submachine gun is the perfect weapon for clearing the confined rooms, corridors, and stairways of the Chancellery building.

127

another hostile at close range in the room above. Once the room is clear, move toward the next stairway.

Pause at the base of the steps and wait for another soldier to move into your sights. When he's down, move up the stairs and immediately turn left to take out a sniper who was peeking through a crack in the wall. Move through the room ahead, past a couple of locked doors, and into a damaged room with a wooden plank spanning a crack in the floor. Go through the door on the other side.

TIP

If you didn't take out the tank below, it may fire at you while you cross the wooden plank. Don't worry, it can't hit you.

This next room contains three soldiers anxious to discover the source of the commotion—don't disappoint them. When all three are down, pick up the first aid kit on the shelf along the eastern wall. The adjoining projection room contains nothing useful. Move to the stairway leading down at the western side of the room. Take out the soldier standing at the bottom of the stairs and go into the hallway.

Turn left and follow the next staircase down. At the bottom, turn around (facing the stairs) and take out the two soldiers who come after you. There's nothing else of interest down here, so go back up the stairs and turn left at the hallway. Pause by the wooden door to your left, but don't enter it. A soldier will come out of one of the side offices down the hall—shoot him. The sound of gunfire draws another soldier out into the hall from the right. Take him down, then enter the room where he was. After entering, turn right to spot the safe.

New Objectives

• Locate the safe combination

• Use combination to open safe

Leave the room with the safe and turn right into the hallway. To the left is a door leading into an office. The safe combination is on the paper sitting on the desk. Press E to pick up the combination.

Head back to the room with the safe. Don't open it yet. As you enter this room, look for the large crack in the outside wall. Equip the SVT 40 and aim through the crack. There's a machine gun nest on the other side of the street in one of the buildings. Pull up the scope's view to get a better look. Once you get your sights lined up, take out the machine gunner. This will make your escape much easier.

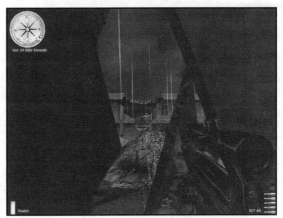

In the room with the safe, look through this crack to find a machine gun nest on the other side of the street.

Turn around and open the safe. Inside are the documents you're looking for—press E to pick them up. Now turn around and peer out the window at the street below. You'll see three German soldiers standing next to a Russian T34. Use the PPSh41 to mow down the soldiers. Time to get out of here.

NEW OBJECTIVE

- Eliminate enemies and commandeer a tank

Make sure you have a full clip in your PPSh41 and rush back into the hallway, turning right. Four German soldiers crowd the hall ahead. Open up with automatic fire until there's nobody left standing in your way. At the end of the hall, follow the stairs down to a room with several lockers. Take out the two soldiers here, then exit through the doors to your left and move toward the T34 to make your escape.

TIP

If you didn't take out the machine gun nest and the three soldiers from the room with the safe, you'll have to contend with these threats before the mission ends.

129

The Empire Falls

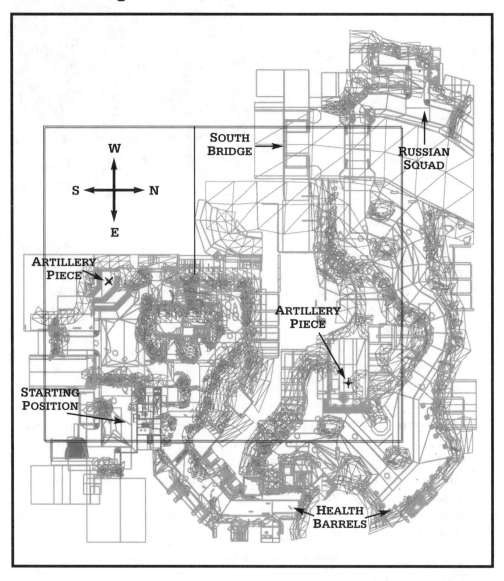

You've located the documents, now comes the hard part—getting out of the city alive. It took longer than you would have liked to find the papers, and now the first wave of Allied bombers is roaring above the city. A Russian T34 tank stands ready to transport you out of the city. Use familiar landmarks for guidance as you alternate between firing on enemy tanks with the main turret and picking off scrambling infantry with the tank's rear-mounted machine gun. At last, you reach the bridge crossing where your mission began. In the massive tank battle that ensues, you must destroy two bridges and fend off many tanks until the next Allied bomber wave arrives to finish off the Nazi forces once and for all.

TIP

Remember, the tank and its turret move independently of one another. Use the movement keys to control the tank's movements and the mouse to rotate the turret. The turret can turn 360 degrees while the mounted DTM machine gun has a more limited, forward-facing firing arc.

131

The Escape

NEW OBJECTIVE

- Return to the Soviet recon group

TIP

If you don't take out the two soldiers exiting the Chancellery building, they'll end up shooting at you from behind.

Stop the soldiers exiting the Chancellery building with a shot from the tank's 88mm main gun.

You begin facing west. Move forward a bit while rotating the tank's turret to face the Chancellery building to the north. A couple of soldiers (one with a Panzerschreck) will exit the building in an attempt to stop you. Fire the tank's main gun through the doorway to take out both soldiers.

On the other side of the rubble to the west is a German tank with few soldiers in front of it. You won't be able to fire through the rubble, so begin weaving around it by turning left. There's a soldier firing at you from a building to the south. Use the DTM to gun him down. While moving south along the rubble, rotate the turret to the west, aiming at the enemy tank. As soon as you clear the rubble, fire at the tank. One shot to the turret should take it out. Mop up the soldiers with the DTM. Concentrate on taking out the soldiers with Panzerschrecks first.

TIP

On occasion, one of the Panzerschreck soldiers on the far side of the enemy tank will inadvertently destroy it in his attempts to hit you.

Once the area is clear, move around the destroyed tank and continue west. As you move forward, another tank will approach along a path to the north. Blast it before it can respond. With this path blocked, proceed to the next one just to the right of the steps in front of the ruined church. Down the path to the north is a group of three soldiers standing in a cluster. Begin by firing the main gun in between them, then switch to the DTM to mop up any survivors.

Maneuver around the rubble to get a clear shot at the enemy tank on the other side.

Move forward, then turn down the next path leading to the southeast. Stop as a halftrack turns in front of you and another tank appears in the distance. Take out the halftrack and then open up on the tank—it should only take one hit before exploding. Once they're taken care of, continue southeast but rotate the turret to the right. Three more soldiers are waiting to ambush you. While moving, mow them down with the DTM.

> ### TIP
> The DTM's extreme recoil makes it difficult to fire accurately. Use short, controlled bursts instead of sweeping across targets with automatic fire. This is especially important when firing at distant targets.

133

Continue to the archway next to the Chancellery building's entrance. Are things looking familiar? A couple of planes will fly through the arch as you approach. Through the arch down the street to the northeast, spot a Panzerschreck soldier on a balcony above the right side of the street. Quickly fire the main gun at him and watch the building's front wall crumble.

Watch out for soldiers equipped with Panzerschrecks positioned along this street.

Continue through the arch while aiming the main gun down the street. Keep the pile of rubble to your left—there's another tank on the other side. As you inch forward, a halftrack comes down the road and stops—ignore it and the tank for now. While you're protected by the rubble, aim down the street until you see a soldier with a Panzerschreck standing at the far end in front of a gray building. Use the main gun to take him out and watch the building behind him collapse.

TIP

When faced with incoming Panzerschreck rounds, continue moving. The rockets travel slowly, allowing you some time to get out of the way.

134

Use the rubble for cover, peeking out to take shots until the enemy tank explodes.

By now, the tank on the other side of the rubble pile is firing at you. Be patient. Stay up against the rubble pile and fire at the halftrack down the street. It may take a couple of shots to destroy it. Back up near the archway to get a clear shot, the rubble gets in the way.

Now turn your attention to the tank. As soon as he fires, move forward and take a shot while his gun's reloading. Immediately back up behind the rubble again before he can get an open shot at you. Wait for him to fire again from behind the rubble, then move forward to take him out. The rest of the street is now clear. Move to the far end and pick up some barrels with red crosses on them. These work like a first aid kit, repairing your tank.

Halfway Home

After picking up the barrels, move through the rubble-filled alley to the west. You'll spot another tank moving in front of you from left to right. Keep moving while firing at the tank ahead, and quickly turn the corner to your right—there's another tank moving in behind you. Go completely around the corner to the right and wait for the sound of an incoming Allied plane— it'll take out the tank behind you.

Take out this tank while moving through the alley. Keep moving—another tank is coming up right behind you!

135

You'll recognize this area as the open courtyard where you retrieved the map from the downed aircraft. Although you cleared it earlier, it's swarming with enemies again. Take it slowly, eliminating one threat at a time. Move north toward the courtyard and open up with the DTM, firing at the Panzerschreck soldier dead ahead.

Despite your efforts, the courtyard is bristling with enemy activity, including a surprise entry by this Tiger Tank.

Pause near the benches and wait for another tank to come into view from the east—one well-placed shot is enough to take it out. Continue moving forward while turning your turret to the west. Take out the three soldiers near the building with the pillars.

Immediately turn the turret forward (facing north) to take out three more soldiers firing at you with mixed ordnance. Move around the right of the charred chassis of the tank ahead. About this time a Tiger Tank will burst through a building to the northeast. Try to get a top hit on the turret to knock it out with one shot.

TIP

Don't worry about taking too much damage in the open courtyard. You can repair the tank once you clear the area by driving over to the barrels in the southeast. However, wait until you clear the area near the river before coming back to repair the tank.

136

Continue moving west (toward the downed aircraft) and turn left around the pile of rubble. Stop and use the DTM to gun down a few soldiers along the road to the west. A halftrack will approach from the same direction. Switch to the main gun to take it out.

Don't forget to use these barrels to repair your tank before leaving the courtyard.

Mop up the remaining troops along the road and backtrack to the far southeast side of the courtyard, where you'll find another stack of barrels to repair the tank. Move back to the road leading west and be ready to engage more infantry. You'll receive new orders as you make your way toward the river.

NEW OBJECTIVE

- Destroy the south bridge

Switch between the main gun and the DTM to take out the troops along the river. A tank will approach from the south and stop on the other side of a pile of rubble. As you did earlier, wait until he fires a shot into the rubble, then rush forward and blow him away with one shell. You should now be able to see the two bridges off to the southwest. You need to take out the far one where the enemy tank is sitting.

Fire at the south bridge and watch the tank fall into the river.

137

First, take out a Panzerschreck soldier on the far west span of the bridge. Follow the rocket contrails to his position and open fire with the DTM. Next, approach the lower north bridge and take out one more soldier. From this position, you should have a good view of the south bridge. The tank on the bridge above appears to be unoccupied, so don't worry about shooting it. Instead, fire at the south bridge with the main gun. This will blow away a chunk of the center span, causing the tank to fall into the river below. Cross the bridge and turn right to meet up with your comrades.

The Last Stand

NEW OBJECTIVE

• Defend the bridge until air support arrives

TIP

To maximize your team's efficiency, fire at the tanks your allies aren't targeting.

As soon as you approach the Russian soldiers near the truck, you get new orders to hold the bridge you just crossed from an incoming assault of German armor. Back up the tank facing east, with the left side near the truck. Two more T34s move in to assist, covering your right flank. Enemy tanks approach across the river from the east, as well as along the south bridge you just damaged. The T34s to your right help you

Watch out for the tanks on the bridge to the south. Their elevated position gives them a significant advantage.

engage the enemy tanks, but they're most useful for attracting incoming rounds while you sit back and fire on the enemy.

Concentrate on taking out the first couple of tanks across the river first, then turn your attention to the bridge to the south. You need to clear the bridge as fast as possible. The enemy tanks are firing from an elevated position, allowing them to score critical hits against you and your allies.

Keep firing while scanning the east and south for new targets. By the end of the battle you'll probably be the lone surviving tank. Kick back while the Russian bombers move in to finish the job. Good work, soldier!

> **TIP**
> While waiting for shells to load, switch to the DTM and help the Russian soldiers engage the enemy infantry across the river.

When it's all over, the Russian bombers will move in overhead to pulverize the city

139

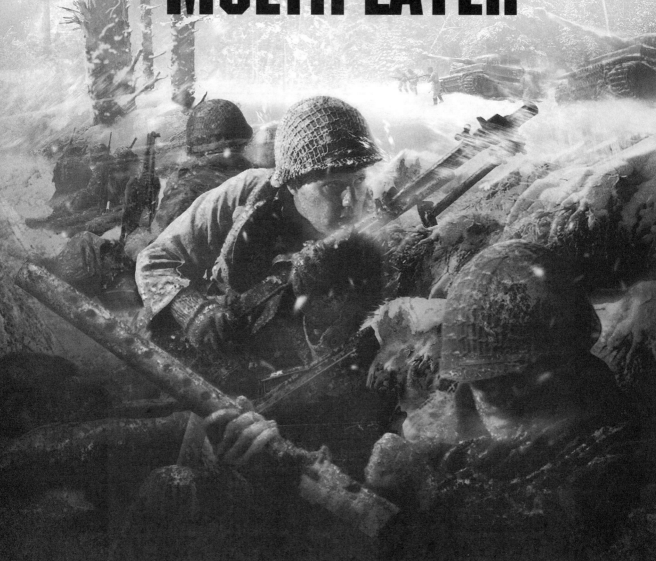

6
MULTIPLAYER

The *Spearhead* expansion adds twelve new maps, providing a breath of fresh air to a game with an established online following. Included are a few maps utilizing the new Tug of War mode (TOW). These maps require teamwork to capture and hold several control points. In this chapter, we take a look at each of the maps, but first let's talk about the basics of multiplayer gaming.

Multiplayer for Beginners

Joining an already established community can be an intimidating experience. But it doesn't have to be that way. In this section we look at ways to fit in and have fun without drawing the ire of your online peers.

Getting Started

Even if you're new to online gaming, you don't want to announce that fact to the world. Start off by creating an online persona. This doesn't have to be anything profound, just a nickname or something unique. Avoid using offensive monikers or anything that draws attention to yourself. Once you've come up with something appropriate, enter it in the Multiplayer Options section.

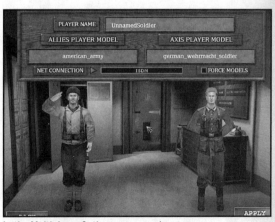

In the Multiplayer Options, you can change your name and the default models.

141

At the top of the screen, enter your online persona in the green box next to "Player Name." If you enter a game as "UnnamedSoldier," everyone will know you're a newbie.

Now select models for both Allies and Axis. This is how your character appears in the game. For the most part, it doesn't matter which model you choose for each side. But if you know you're going to play on a particular map, spend time browsing through the available models. For example, if you know you'll be playing on a map with snow, picking one of the models with winter camouflage makes you harder to see. In most cases, the maps rotate. So what makes you hard to see on one map makes you stand out on another. It's best to choose something neutral along the darker tones.

From the same screen, select your Net connection. You may not find the appropriate setting to describe your connection, so just pick the closest option. An accurate setting isn't required for joining a game, but it helps adjust your system to improve online performance. When you're done, click the "Apply" button at the bottom.

TIP

To use the new weapons, select a British or Soviet model.

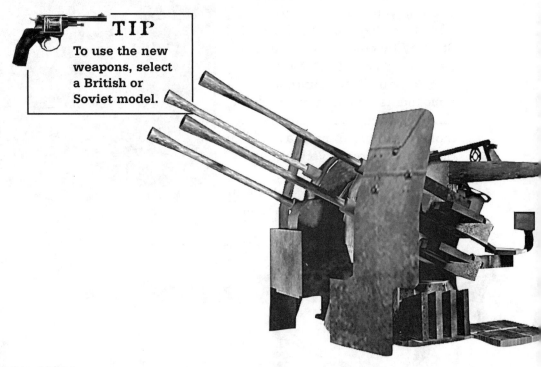

142

Next, find a server. Exit to the main Multiplayer screen and select the Join Game section. If you want to find a game on the Internet, click the appropriate buttons until you come to an option that says "Browse Internet Servers." Click on this button to open the server browser window. At the bottom of the screen, click on the "Update Server" button. This downloads a list of available games currently being played online. Look for a server with a few people on it and a low ping. Ideally, you'll want to find a ping below 100, but this may vary depending on your location and method of connection. Once you find a game, highlight the game, then click the "Join Game" button at the bottom of the screen. You'll now attempt to join the game in progress.

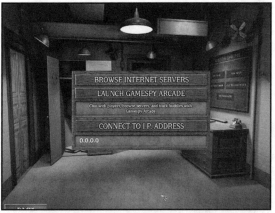

Choose "Browse Internet Servers" to find an online game.

Browse through the available games until you find one that looks good.

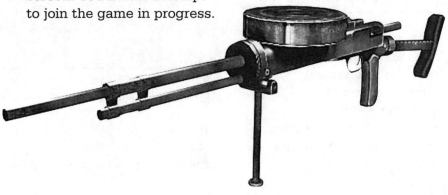

Watch and Learn

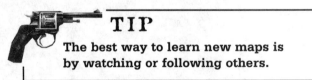

TIP

The best way to learn new maps is by watching or following others.

Even if you're a veteran of other online shooters, there's still a steep learning curve in becoming familiar with the new maps. Whenever possible, join a team-style game—this way only half the players will try to kill you. Once you're in the game, move as whizzing bullets and explosions contribute to the chaos of the online battlefield. Find a teammate and follow him into action—if he's moving, chances are he knows what he's doing. While following, keep an eye open for enemies and offer fire support when needed. You may not last a long time, but following and helping teammates is the best way to become acquainted with a map. Keep this up until you feel comfortable to move out on your own.

Everyone plays the game differently. Just by watching others, you can become a better player yourself by analyzing what works and what doesn't.

Etiquette

Problem players can be voted off the server by calling a vote. Choose the "Kick Client" option.

TIP

The game isn't a chat room, so keep unrelated topics to a minimum.

For the most part, other players are courteous and willing to help out newbies. After all, it's the influx of new players that keeps the community alive and growing. However, once in a while, you'll come across a player who wants to be the center of attention. Although he may be extremely annoying, the best thing to do is

144

ignore him. Unfortunately, situations like this often result in shouting matches between a few players while everybody else tries to stay focused on the game. Remember, the game is not a chat room. Everything you type goes out to each player, eating up precious bandwidth in the process. It's not very considerate to subject your fellow players to long-winded messages that ultimately distract them from the gaming experience. Even if you feel personally offended, this isn't the appropriate place to defend yourself. Instead, redirect your rage into the game in an attempt to hunt down the offending player. There's nothing more cathartic than blasting a loudmouth with a full auto burst.

TIP

If things get too far out of hand, consider voting a problem player off. Your fellow gamers will be more than happy to place a vote to kick out a troublemaker.

Team Play

Lately, multiplayer games have become more team based. This requires more cooperation and effective communication than the more traditional death match games. In team-based games, players are challenged with working together to achieve particular goals. This presents new problems to gamers who take care of themselves. Not only do they have to learn to work with others, they'll have to analyze the current situation and formulate the appropriate strategy to best serve the team. More than any other game type, the new Tug of War mode demands cooperative team play, so brush up on the basics.

145

Communication

> ### TIP
>
> When communicating with teammates,
> use the compass to help specify directions.

Effective communication is the best way to get a team to work together. In highly organized team-play games, one player is designated as a team leader who issues the commands to the team. But in most team-play games there's no real chain of command in place. This can result in confusing radio chatter as your teammates issue conflicting orders and report erroneous information.

Although you can't control the actions of your teammates, you can ensure your communications are clear and concise. It may sound obvious, but focus on relaying messages that have relevance to the current situation. Some players continuously repeat the same message just to hear themselves talk. Not only is this annoying, but it's akin to crying wolf.

> ### TIP
>
> Type messages to your teammates by
> pressing T to open the team chat option.
> To type messages to everyone in the game,
> press Y. However, use these options sparingly.
> You can't move while typing, making you
> a sitting duck.

The best way to communicate is with the prerecorded voice messages. You can access these by pressing V. This brings up a menu of five message options. Behind these options are 40 canned messages that can be sent through this pop-up menu system. Instead of typing out each command, all you have to do is open the voice menu, select the message type, then find the appropriate phrase. After

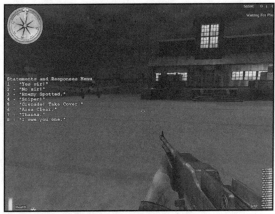

The voice message menu provides enough canned phrases to keep your team informed.

three short key strokes, you've sent your message, allowing you to turn your attention back to the battlefield. As you can see below, there are more than enough phrases to explain any tactical situation.

GOAL MESSAGES

KEY	MESSAGE
1	"Good job team!"
2	"Alright!"
3	"We've done it!"
4	"Woohoo!"
5	"Objective achieved."
6	"We've completed an objective."
7	"We've lost an objective!"
8	"The enemy has overrun our objective!"

147

SQUAD COMMANDS

KEY	MESSAGE
1	"Squad, move in!"
2	"Squad, fall back!"
3	"Squad, attack right flank!"
4	"Squad, attack left flank!"
5	"Squad, hold this position!"
6	"Squad, covering fire!"
7	"Squad, regroup!"
8	"Squad, split up!"

INDIVIDUAL COMMANDS

KEY	MESSAGE
1	"Cover me!"
2	"I'll cover you!"
3	"Follow me!"
4	"You take point!"
5	"Taking fire! Need some help!"
6	"Get ready to move in on my signal."
7	"Attack!"
8	"Open fire!"

STATEMENTS AND RESPONSES

KEY	MESSAGE
1	"Yes sir!"
2	"No sir!"
3	"Enemy spotted."
4	"Sniper!"
5	"Grenade! Take cover!"
6	"Area clear."
7	"Thanks."
8	"I owe you one."

TAUNTS

KEY	MESSAGE
1	"Who wants more?!"
2	"Never send boys to do a man's job."
3	"This is too easy!"
4	"You mess with the best, you die like the rest."
5	"Watch that friendly fire!"
6	"Hey, I'm on your team!"
7	"Come on out, you cowards!"
8	"Where are you hiding?"

149

Assault

> ## TIP
>
> Take notice whether friendly fire is on or not. If it's on, you'll be able to inflict damage on your teammates. Be particularly careful when throwing grenades.

Whether you need to take an objective or eliminate the other side, your team will need to stage successful assaults. It's important to choose the right kind of weapon. Machine guns and submachine guns are your best choice for these operations. Have at least one heavy weapon in your assault force. Choose a bazooka or Panzerschreck, but don't move while they're equipped—they slow you down too much. With practice, sniper rifles are effective, but they're also difficult because you'll need to stop to line up your sights—you don't want to stop during an assault. If you want to use a sniper rifle, cover your team's movements from a distance while concealed.

> ## TIP
>
> More often than not, a team's performance is hindered by an overabundance of snipers. Your team rarely needs more than a couple of snipers at a time. Instead, concentrate on assaulting and defending with more versatile weapons.

When possible, gather a group of four or five teammates before moving out. While approaching an objective, keep an even spread between yourself and your teammates. This makes you less vulnerable to grenade and other attacks. This also applies when taking cover. If you crowd in behind one another, all it takes is one

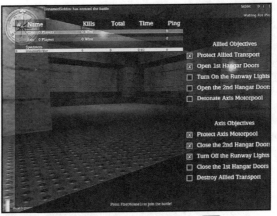

Check up on your team objectives by pressing Tab.

grenade to bring your assault to an abrupt end. Once an objective is secured, leave someone behind to defend it while your team moves on to the next goal.

TIP

Unlike single-player games, you can drop weapons in multiplayer games. This allows you to pick up different weapons from downed enemies or teammates. To drop your weapon, press H.

Defend

There's nothing more disheartening than successfully assaulting an enemy position, and subsequently losing it because no one defended it. Defending may be less important in other game types, but it is a significant element of your team strategy during Tug of War matches. The number of teammates needed for defending a position fluctuates throughout the course of a game based on necessity.

151

Therefore, study the ever-
changing balance of power,
and concentrate on
defending the appropriate
positions at the right times.
In general, keep at least
one teammate behind to
defend. At the very least,
they'll be able to report
when they're under attack.

Choosing the appropriate
weapon for defense is
just as important as your
selections for assault. If you

Mountable weapons such as this AA gun are
useful for defense.

plan on physically holding the position, you need the brute firepower
of machine guns and other heavy weapons. But if you plan on
watching it from a distance, use a sniper rifle and hide within view
of the objective. However, if you decide to use this tactic, the
objective may be captured by the enemy. So be quick to move out of
your hiding spot to recapture it once the attackers are eliminated.

Utilize the mountable weapons surrounding the objective. This
can range from machine gun nests to AA guns. If you decide to use
these weapons, make sure you're protected from flanking attacks
and concentrate your fire along predictable paths.

Tug of War Maps
Ardennes

Allied Objectives

- Protect transport
- Keep main gate open
- Control the flak 88
- Shut down Axis generator
- Detonate the Axis bunker

The Allies need to open the gate ahead to gain direct
entry to the village.

PRIMAGAMES.COM

Ardennes

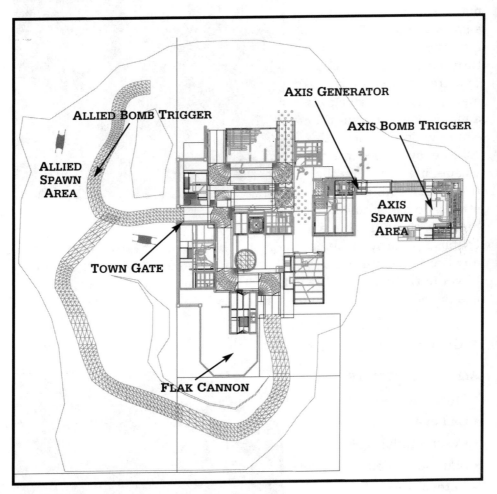

AXIS OBJECTIVES

- Protect the bunker
- Stop generator shutdown
- Control the flak 88
- Close main gate
- Destroy Allied transport

Like most of the TOW maps, this night fight in a snow-dusted village requires the Axis forces to turn back an Allied force. The area surrounding the main gate to the village is a major point of contention. Not only does it allow the Allies easy access into the village, it also makes their transport vulnerable to attack. To assist in its defense, the Allies have a

There's a portable MG-42 in this church tower.

couple of nearby machine gun nests that should be used to prevent any German counterattacks. There's a portable MG-42 in the high tower in the center of the village. The Germans stand a better chance of getting to it before the Allies.

Berlin

ALLIED OBJECTIVES

- Protect ammo depot
- Call in air support
- Control radar dish
- Shut down flak 88
- Detonate Axis ammo depot

Expect heavy activity in the large courtyard with the flak 88 and the radar dish.

154

Berlin

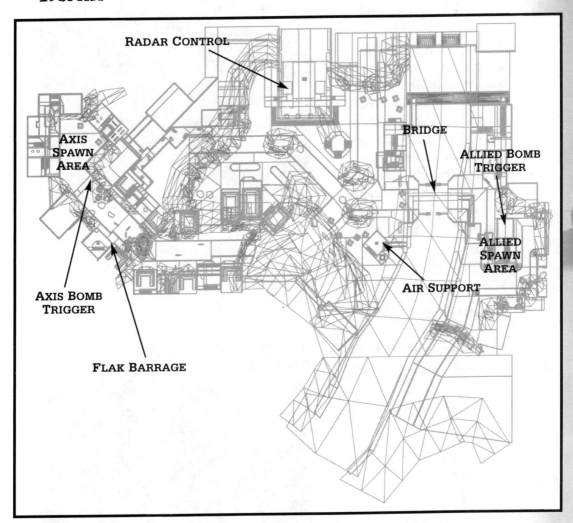

RADAR CONTROL

AXIS
SPAWN
AREA

BRIDGE

ALLIED BOMB
TRIGGER

ALLIED
SPAWN
AREA

AIR SUPPORT

AXIS BOMB
TRIGGER

FLAK BARRAGE

AXIS OBJECTIVES

- Protect ammo depot
- Start flak 88 barrage
- Control radar dish
- Call off Allied air support
- Destroy Allied ammo depot

155

At the start of this game, the Axis and Allied forces are on an even footing, making for a frantic first few minutes as each side tries to establish control. The team that controls the large courtyard (with the radar dish) stands a good chance of pulling off a victory. But it's a large area to defend, so the controlling force should concentrate their fire at

A portable MG-42 can be found in the Allied ammo depot.

entry areas. The Allies approach from the West, while the Axis forces move through the alley to the East. This time, the Allies start with the portable MG-42 in their ammo depot.

Druckammern

ALLIED OBJECTIVES

- Protect the transport
- Disengage U-boat clamps
- Open pen doors
- Steal U-boat
- Detonate German entrance

AXIS OBJECTIVES

- Protect entrance
- Close pen doors
- Engage U-boat clamps
- Prevent U-boat theft
- Destroy Allied transport

The crates surrounding the U-boat provide good places to hide once the shooting starts.

Druckammern

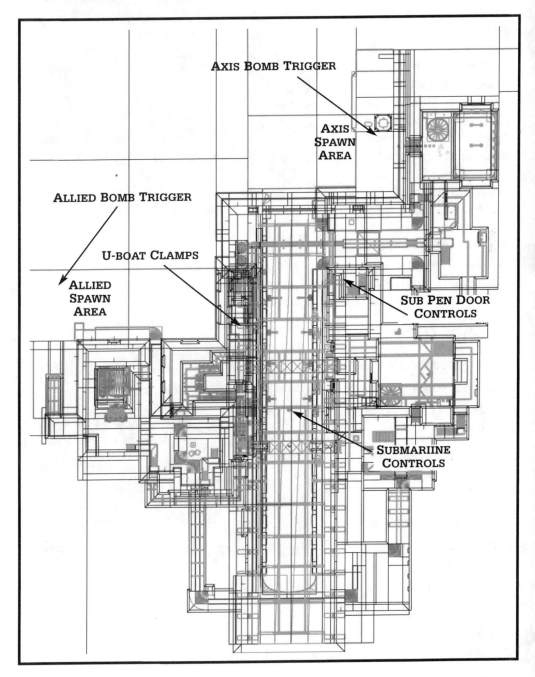

AXIS BOMB TRIGGER

AXIS SPAWN AREA

ALLIED BOMB TRIGGER

U-BOAT CLAMPS

ALLIED SPAWN AREA

SUB PEN DOOR CONTROLS

SUBMARIINE CONTROLS

157

The Allies have their work cut out for them. Not only do they have to steal an enemy U-boat, but they have to keep some forces back to protect their transport. The twisting corridors of the sub pen make them ideal for Axis ambushes. Fortunately, there are multiple ways to get around, which leads to the Axis forces spreading themselves a little thin. Still, the Allies need to coordinate their assault carefully to get away with the enemy U-boat. The closed pen doors and the engaged U-boat clamps must be addressed before the theft is a success.

The sub pen doors need to be opened before the Allies can get away with the sub.

Flughafen

ALLIED OBJECTIVES

- Protect Allied transport
- Open first hangar doors
- Turn on runway lights
- Open second hangar doors
- Detonate Axis motor pool

AXIS OBJECTIVES

- Protect Axis Motor Pool
- Close the second hangar doors
- Turn off the runway lights
- Close the first hangar doors
- Destroy Allied transport

Watch out for enemy snipers while crossing the wide-open spaces.

Flughafen

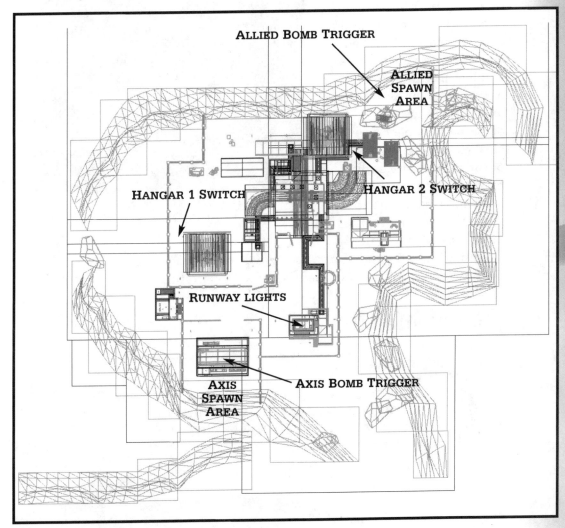

ALLIED BOMB TRIGGER

ALLIED SPAWN AREA

HANGAR 1 SWITCH

HANGAR 2 SWITCH

RUNWAY LIGHTS

AXIS BOMB TRIGGER

AXIS SPAWN AREA

159

This desert airfield is large, requiring both sides to cross open terrain and making it an ideal map to unleash your snipers on. However, you'll still want a good mix of weapons for assaulting and defending the objectives. Expect heavy clashes around the center of the map in the early minutes of the game as both sides scramble to secure objectives on the other side of the airfield.

Look between these trucks to find the spot to place explosives to destroy the Axis motor pool.

Hold back and defend your already held objectives, then counterattack once you defeat the enemies' first assault.

Other Maps

NOTE

The TOW maps can also be played in Free for All, Team, and Round Based matches. However, the objectives will be disabled.

Bahnhof

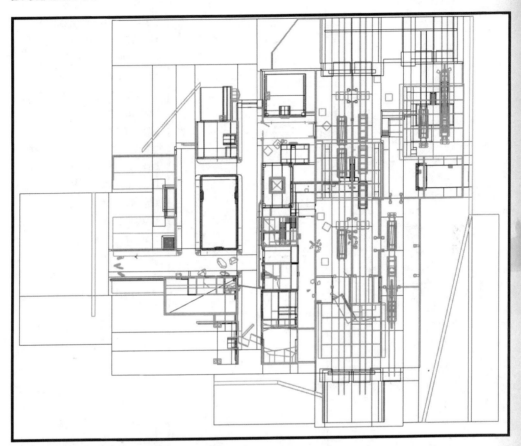

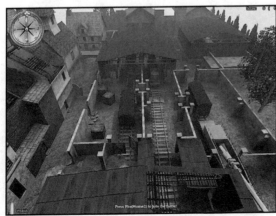

This maze-like trainyard makes for some exciting surprises as you move around corners.

This train station map has a really tight layout, ideal for fast-paced death match games. Submachine guns come in handy on this one. Compared to the trainyard, the city portion (to the South) is open, offering clear fields of fire for snipers and other long rifles. These two areas provide a nice contrast.

161

Bazaar

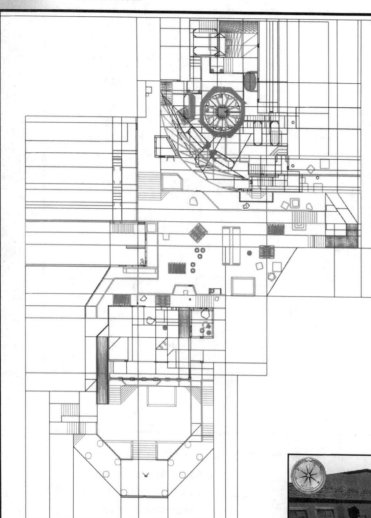

The multi-tiered Bazaar makes for an interesting mix of close- and medium-range combat. Watch out for enemy machine gunners and snipers on the various balconies. They make moving across the open areas of the market a bit dangerous. Use cover and watch out for incoming grenades. When possible, stay on the upper levels.

The balconies make the market below a dangerous killing zone. Notice the portable MG-42 on the balcony to the right. There's another one on the opposite side of the courtyard.

Brest

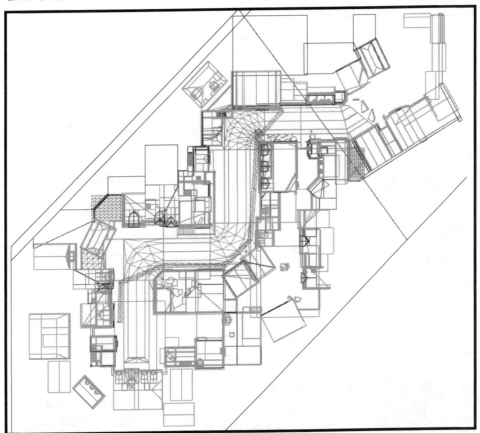

Spotting snipers in this cluttered city can be tough. Use the destroyed vehicles for cover.

If urban combat is your thing, you can't go wrong with Brest. The rubble and destroyed vehicles provide good cover as you move through the streets. There are also tight interiors that offer close-quarter opportunities. Look out for snipers along the high, exposed areas above the streets.

163

Gewitter

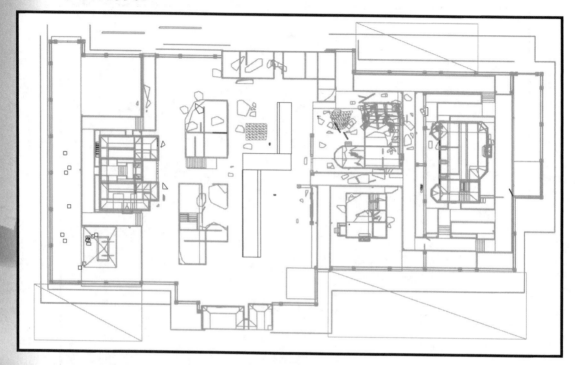

Another urban map with the addition of several weapon positions, such as this mortar.

This large map is great for big team matches. The mortar and machine gun positions offer a variety of defensive opportunities. But be careful when manning these weapons. They are exposed, making you a vulnerable and highly visible target.

Holland

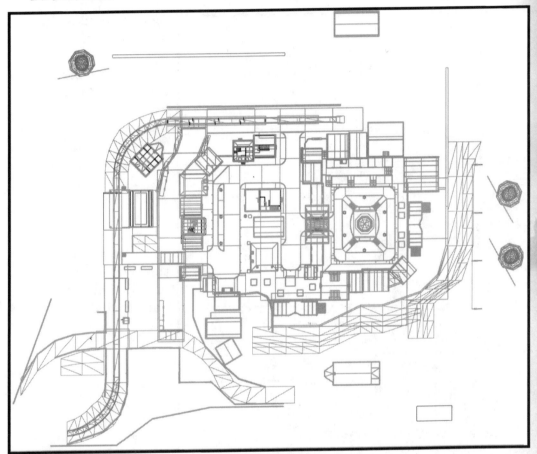

Finally! A town that isn't a smoldering heap of rubble!

Compared to the other urban maps, this one offers a nice change of scenery. Moving along the train (sitting on the tracks to the West) allows you to move from one end of the map to the other without exposing yourself to the open streets where solid cover is sparse.

165

Stadt

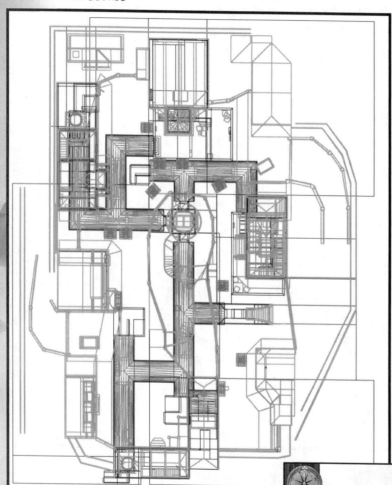

Rich in detail and surprises, this map has a variety of paths that make it great for large-scale death match engagements. The subterranean passageways give you the chance to pop up in a variety of places, making campers paranoid. Keep moving on this map—good hiding spots are hard to find.

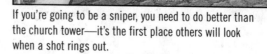

If you're going to be a sniper, you need to do better than the church tower—it's the first place others will look when a shot rings out.

Unterseite

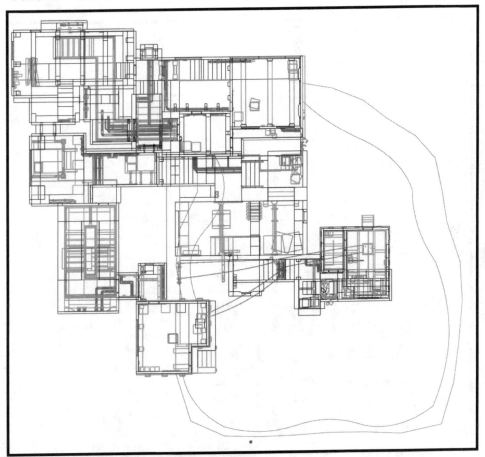

The claustrophobic nature of this level makes automatic weapons a must.

This underground industrial map has all the ingredients for fast-paced death match games. The halls and rooms are small enough for exciting gun battles, yet big enough to avoid incoming grenades. When entering new rooms, check out all the corners—there are several platforms that campers will love to snipe from.

167

Verschneit

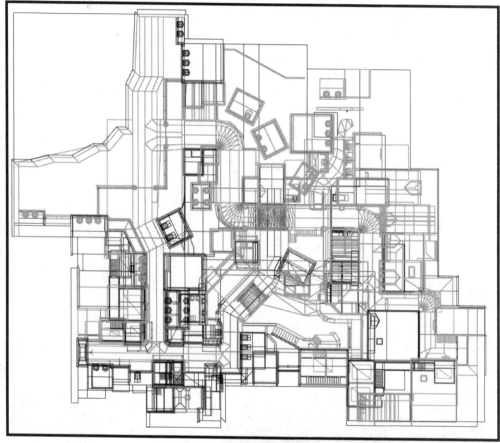

This large urban map with a good mix of close-quarter interiors and wide-open exteriors is an excellent choice for large team games. Despite the numerous balconies, there aren't that many concealed sniping positions—but don't let your guard down.

The long, narrow streets make long-distance engagements a common occurrence in this urban setting.

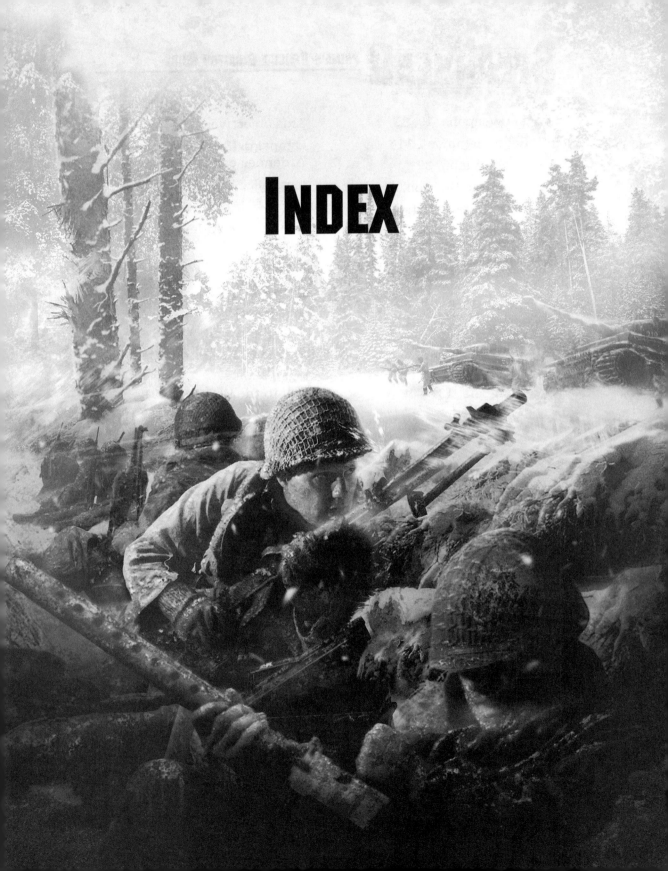

INDEX

171

174

175

M

177

R

S

179

181

183

BEAT THE WORLD,
One Level At A Time

With so many levels to conquer, **you need a plan.** Information about what's coming, what's here, what's now; tips and strategies from the inside, cheats **direct from the source...**

That's **EAGAMES.com,** where you'll find the latest demos, movies you just can't get anywhere else, screenshots direct from the game makers, and official information about every available EA GAMES title. All in one place, only at *eagames.com*

Challenge Everything™

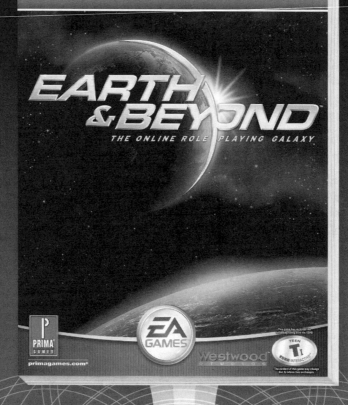

WE'VE GOT STRATEGY COVERED